A BIBLIOGRAPHY
OF STUDIES IN
METAPHYSICAL POETRY
1939-1960

A BIBLIOGRAPHY
OF STUDIES IN
METAPHYSICAL POETRY
1939-1960

Compiled by Lloyd E. Berry

MADISON, 1964

THE UNIVERSITY OF WISCONSIN PRESS

FOR EDNA PAYNE CASKEY

PREFACE

This Bibliography of Studies in Metaphysical Poetry, 1939—
1960 is intended to be a continuation of Theodore Spencer's
bibliography published in 1939. Mr. T. S. Eliot long ago, in
1931 to be exact, predicted studies in Metaphysical Poets
(and particularly in Donne) had reached their zenith. Even
Mr. Spencer suggested a saturation point had been reached
in Donne scholarship. Yet since the 1930's, scholarship on
the Metaphysical Poets has greatly multiplied, not dimin-
ished. Along with a certain amount of "busy work," there
have been such significant contributions as editions of the
works of Herbert, Carew, Traherne, and the magnificent edition of Donne's sermons. It would be a dangerous thing
to single out any one study for special commendation, so
I will, with Chaucer, declare that the reader "shal fynde
ynowe, grete and smale."

I have attempted to make the present bibliography as
complete as possible, within certain limits mentioned be-
low; but I am only too well aware of possible omissions,
and I would be very grateful to any reader who would call
to my attention an omitted item.

Under the heading of "General Studies," only items
that have particular relevance to the study of Metaphysical poetry have been included. Under individual poets, I
have listed editions of works, but I have not listed any
anthologies in which their poems may appear. Revised editions of works but not new issues have been recorded. I
have not noted reviews of any books, as one may consult
the annual bibliography in Studies in Philology for such in-
formation. Biographies of the poets in encyclopedias or
nonce references in literary histories, books, and articles
have not been listed.

PREFACE

It is important for the user of this bibliography to remember that he should consult the "General Studies" section as well as the individual author section in order to have a complete list of material relating to the individual author.

It remains only for me to acknowledge the generous assistance given this project. I am particularly grateful to the American Philosophical Society, who by a grant from the Penrose Fund, enabled me to complete the bibliography at an earlier date than would otherwise have been possible. The Research Board of the University of Illinois granted funds for research assistants, and Lindsay Mann, Dennis Donovan, and John Via have rendered yeoman service. Mr. Mann and Mr. Donovan worked through periodicals, and Mr. Donovan and Mr. Via also helped with verifying entries and with other such onerous tasks. I am grateful to them for their good-natured tolerance, especially to Mr. Donovan and Mr. Via, who had to work in non-airconditioned stacks during the summer months. Professors Joseph Summers, Muriel C. Bradbrook, Robert B. Hinman, E. L. Marilla, and Rhodes Dunlap kindly read through the sections on Herbert, Marvell, Cowley, Vaughan, and Carew, respectively. Miss Eva Faye Benton, the librarian of the English Library, has, as always, been very helpful in locating books and journals. However, for all errors and omissions I, alone, am responsible.

This bibliography is dedicated to Professor Edna Payne Caskey, who years ago was not content with just persuading a college freshman to change his major to English but also convinced him that teaching might be a worthwhile profession.

Lloyd E. Berry

1 August 1963
University of Illinois
Urbana, Illinois

TABLE OF CONTENTS

ABBREVIATIONS OF TITLES

OF JOURNALS

DA	Dissertation Abstracts
EIC	Essays in Criticism (Oxford)
ELH	Journal of English Literary History
Essays & Studies	Essays & Studies by Members of the English Association
HLQ	Huntington Library Quarterly
JEGP	Journal of English and Germanic Philology
JHI	Journal of the History of Ideas
KR	Kenyon Review
MLN	Modern Language Notes
MLQ	Modern Language Quarterly
MLR	Modern Language Review
MP	Modern Philology
N &Q	Notes and Queries
PBSA	Papers of the Bibliographical Society of America
PMLA	Publications of the Modern Language Association
PQ	Philological Quarterly
RES	Review of English Studies
RN	Renaissance News
SB	Studies in Bibliography
SCN	Seventeenth Century News
SP	Studies in Philology
SR	Sewanee Review
TLS	[London] Times Literary Supplement
UTQ	University of Toronto Quarterly

A BIBLIOGRAPHY
OF STUDIES IN
METAPHYSICAL POETRY
1939-1960

GENERAL STUDIES

1939

Brooks, Cleanth.   Modern Poetry and the Tradition.   0001
Chapel Hill, University of North Carolina.   xi,
253 p.

Praz, Mario.   Studies in Seventeenth-Century Im-   0002
agery.   London, The Warburg Institute, 1939—
1947. 2 v.

Selincourt, Ernest de.   The Interplay of Literature   0003
and Science During the Last Three Centuries.
Hibbert Journal, 37: 225-245.

Spencer, Theodore and Mark Van Doren.   Studies   0004
in Metaphysical Poetry: Two Essays and a Bibliography.   New York, Columbia University.
88 p.

1940

Daniels, R. Balfour.   Some Seventeenth-Century   0005
Worthies in a Twentieth-Century Mirror.   Chapel
Hill, University of North Carolina.   x, 156 p.

Jonas, Leah.   The Divine Science: The Aesthetic   0006
of Some Representative Seventeenth-Century
Poets.   New York, Columbia University. xii,
292 p.

Sharp, Robert L.   From Donne to Dryden: The Re-   0007
volt Against Metaphysical Poetry.   Chapel Hill,
University of North Carolina.   xiii, 221 p.

Shuster, George N.   The English Ode From Milton   0008
to Keats.   New York, Columbia University. vi,
314 p.

GENERAL STUDIES

1941

0009   Daniels, Earl R. K.   The Art of Reading Poetry. New York, Farrar and Rinehart. vii, 519 p.

0010   Mortimer, R.   Metaphysical School of Poetry. New Statesman and Nation, 21: 534.

0011   Ransom, John Crowe.   Eliot and The Metaphysicals. Accent, 1: 148—156.

1942

0012   Brandenburg, Alice S.   The Dynamic Image in Metaphysical Poetry. PMLA, 57: 1039—1045.

0013   James, Eleanor.   The Emblem as an Image-Pattern in Some Metaphysical Poets. Summaries of Doctoral Dissertations, University of Wisconsin, 7: 291—293.

0014   Tuve, Rosemond.   Imagery and Logic: Ramus and Metaphysical Poetics. JHI, 3:365—400.

1944

0015   Grierson, H. J. C. and J. C. Smith.   A Critical History of English Poetry. London, Chatto and Windus. viii, 527 p.

0016   Sypher, Wylie.   The Metaphysicals and the Baroque. Partisan Review, 11: 3—17.

1945

0017   Bush, Douglas.   English Literature in the Earlier Seventeenth Century. Oxford, Clarendon. vi, 621 p.

0018   Fogle, R. H.   Romantic Bards and Metaphysical Reviewers. ELH, 12: 221—250.

0019   Knights, L. C.   On the Social Background of Metaphysical Poetry. Scrutiny, 13: 37—52.

0020   Thoma, Henry F.   The Hermetic Strain in Seventeenth-Century Mysticism. Summaries of Theses, Harvard University, pp. 344—347.

0021   Wilson, F. P.   Elizabethan and Jacobean. Oxford, Clarendon. vi, 144 p.

1946

0022   Doughty, William L.   Studies in Religious Poetry

of the Seventeenth Century. London, Epworth.
xiv, 199 p.

Knights, L. C. Explorations; Essays in Criticism,   0023
Mainly on the Literature of the Seventeenth Century. London, Chatto and Windus. xii, 198 p.

Praz, Mario. Poesia Metafisica Inglese del Sei-   0024
cento. Poesia 3—4: 232—242.

Stegemeier, Henri. Problems in Emblem Literature.   0025
JEGP, 45: 26—37.

Wellek, René. The Concept of Baroque in Literary   0026
Scholarship. Jahrbuch für Amerikastudien, 5:
77—109.

1947

Day Lewis, Cecil. The Poetic Image. New York,   0027
Oxford University. 157 p.

Delattre, Floris. De la Chanson Élizabéthaine au   0028
Poème Métaphysique. Modern Languages (Lon-
don), 28: 91—96.

Milch, Werner. Deutsche Barochlyrik und "Meta-   0029
physical Poetry" in England. Trivium, 5: 65—73.

Tuve, Rosemond. Elizabethan and Metaphysical   0030
Imagery. Chicago, Chicago University. xiv,
442 p.

1948

Freeman, Rosemary. English Emblem Books. Lon-   0031
don, Chatto and Windus. xiv, 256 p.

Husain, Itrat. The Mystical Element in the Meta-   0032
physical Poets of the Seventeenth Century.
Edinburgh, Oliver and Boyd. 351 p.

Miles, Josephine. The Primary Language of Poetry   0033
in the 1640's. Berkeley, University of Cali-
fomia. 160 p.

Mims, Edwin. The Christ of the Poets. New York   0034
and Nashville, Abingdon-Cokesbury. 256 p.

O'Connor, William Van. The Influence of the Met-   0035
aphysicals on Modern Poetry. College English,
9: 180—187.

1949

Boase, Alan M. Poètes Anglais et Français de   0036

GENERAL STUDIES

l'Époque Baroque. Revue des Sciences Humaines, nos. 55—56: 155—184.

0037 Danby, John F. The Poets on Fortune's Hill: Literature and Society, 1580—1610. Cambridge Journal, 2: 195—211.

0038 Grierson, H. J. C. Criticism and Creation: Essays and Addresses. London, Chatto and Windus. viii, 127 p.

0039 Gros, Léon-Gabriel. Métaphysique Anglais, du Raisonnement en Poésie. Cahiers du Sud, 29: 3—30.

0040 Tate, Allen. Johnson on the Metaphysicals. KR, 11: 379—394.

1950

0041 Arms, George W. and Joseph M. Kuntz. Poetry Explication: A Checklist of Interpretation Since 1925 of British and American Poets Past and Present. New York, Swallow and Morrow. 187 p.

0042 Bush, Douglas. Science and English Poetry: A Historical Sketch, 1590—1950. New York, Oxford University. viii, 166 p.

0043 Keast, William R. Johnson's Criticism of the Metaphysical Poets. ELH, 17: 59—70.

0044 Mahood, M. M. Poetry and Humanism. London, Jonathan Cape. 335 p.

0045 Nicolson, Marjorie H. The Breaking of the Circle: Studies in the Effect of the "New Science" Upon Seventeenth Century Poetry. Evanston, Northwestern University. xxii, 193 p. Revised edition: New York, Columbia University, 1960. xi, 216 p.

0046 Wallerstein, Ruth. Studies in Seventeenth Century Poetic. Madison, University of Wisconsin. x, 421 p.

0047 Wedgwood, C. V. Seventeenth-Century English Literature. London, Oxford University. v, 186 p.

1951

0048 Bateson, F. W. Dissociation of Sensibility. EIC, 1: 302-312.

GENERAL STUDIES

Bethell, S. L.   The Cultural Revolution of the   0049
Seventeenth Century.   London, D. Dobson. 161 p.
Mazzeo, Joseph A.   Aspects of Wit and Science in   0050
the Renaissance.   DA, 11: 114—115.
Mazzeo, Joseph A.   A Seventeenth-Century Theory   0051
of Metaphysical Poetry.   Romanic Review, 42:
245—255.

1952

Baker, Herschel.   The Wars of Truth.   Cambridge,   0052
Harvard University.   xi, 390 p.
Bamborough, J. B.   The Little World of Man.   Lon-   0053
don, Longmans, Green.   187 p.
Danby, John F.   Poets on Fortune's Hill: Studies   0054
in Sidney, Shakespeare, Beaumont and Fletcher.
London, Faber and Faber.   212 p.
Mazzeo, Joseph A.   A Critique of Some Modern   0055
Theories of Metaphysical Poetry.   MP, 50: 88—
96.
Raiziss, Sona.   The Metaphysical Passion: Seven   0056
Modern American Poets and the Seventeenth
Century Tradition.   Philadelphia, University of
Pennsylvania.   xv, 327 p.
Ross, Malcolm M.   Analogy and Metaphor: A Note   0057
on the Decline of the Metaphysical Style.   SCN,
10: 13.
Smith, Harold W.   The Dissociation of Sensibility.   0058
Scrutiny, 18: 175—188.
Thomson, Patricia.   The Literature of Patronage,   0059
1580—1630.   EIC, 2: 267—284.
Wiley, Margaret L.   The Subtle Knot: Creative   0060
Scepticism in Seventeenth-Century England.
London, G. Allen and Unwin.   303 p.

1953

Addison, James Thayer.   Early Anglican Thought,   0061
1559—1667.   Historical Magazine of the Prot-
estant Episcopal Church, 22: 248—369.
Bennett, Joan.   Four Metaphysical Poets.   2nd edn.   0062
Cambridge, Cambridge University.   ix, 126 p.
Bethell, S. L.   Gracián, Tesauro, and the Nature   0063
of Metaphysical Wit.   Northern Miscellany of

7

GENERAL STUDIES

Literary Criticism, 1: 19—40.

0064   Collmer, Robert G.   The Concept of Death in the
Poetry of Donne, Herbert, Crashaw, and Vaughan.
DA, 13: 804—805.

0065   Duncan, Joseph E.   The Revival of Metaphysical
Poetry. PMLA, 68: 658—671.

0066   Hart, E. F.   Caroline Lyrics and Contemporary
Song-Books. The Library, 5th ser., 8: 89—110.

0067   McCann, Eleanor M.   The Influence of Sixteenth
and Seventeenth Century Spanish Mystics and
Ascetics on Some Metaphysical Writers. DA, 13:
229—230.

0068   Malloch, A. E.   The Unified Sensibility and Metaphysical Poetry. College English, 15: 95—101.

0069   Mazzeo, Joseph A.   Metaphysical Poetry and the
Poetic of Correspondence, JHI, 14: 221—234.

0070   Mourgues, Odette de.   Metaphysical, Baroque and
Précieux Poetry. Oxford, Clarendon. vii, 184 p.

0071   Pellegrini, Giuliano.   Barocco Inglese. Messina,
Casa Editrice G. D'Anna. 245 p.

0072   Perkins, David.   Johnson on Wit and Metaphysical
Poetry. ELH, 20: 200—217.

0073   Ross, Malcolm M.   A Note on the Metaphysicals.
Hudson Review, 6: 106—113.

0074   Watkin, E. I.   Poets and Mystics. London, Sheed
and Ward. ix, 318 p.

1954

0075   Cruttwell, Patrick.   The Shakespearean Moment
and Its Place in the Poetry of the Seventeenth
Century. London, Chatto and Windus. 262 p.

0076   Cunningham, James V.   Logic and Lyric. MP, 51:
33—41.

0077   Lewis, C. S.   English Literature in the Sixteenth
Century. Oxford, Clarendon. vi, 696 p.

0078   Martz, Louis L.   The Poetry of Meditation: A Study
in English Religious Literature of the Seventeenth
Century. New Haven, Yale. xiv, 375 p.

1955

0079   Esch, Arno.   Englische Religiöse Lyrik des 17. Jahr-
hunderts. Studien zu Donne, Herbert, Crashaw,

8

GENERAL STUDIES

Vaughan. Tubingen, Max Niemeyer Verlag. xi, 225 p.

Groom, Bernard. The Diction of Poetry from Spenser to Bridges. Toronto, Toronto University. viii, 284 p.   0080

Symes, Gordon. The Paradoxes of Poetry. English (London), 8: 69—73.   0081

Walton, Geoffrey. Metaphysical to Augustan. London, Bowes and Bowes. xi, 160 p.   0082

Warnke, Frank J. Marino and the English Metaphysicals. Studies in the Renaissance, 2: 160—175.   0083

Watson, George. Hobbes and the Metaphysical Conceit. JHI, 16: 558—562.   0084

1956

Cornelius, David K. The Caustic Muse: A Study in Seventeenth-Century Verse Satire. DA, 16: 747.   0085

Denonain, Jean-Jacques. Thèmes et formes de la poésie "métaphysique": Étude d'un aspect de la littérature anglaise au dix-septième siècle. Paris, Presses Universitaires de France. 548 p.   0086

Ford, Boris. From Donne to Marvell. Vol. 3 of A Guide to English Literature (Pelican Book). London, Penguin Books. 277 p.   0087

Gang, T. M. Hobbes and the Metaphysical Conceit: A Reply. JHI, 17: 418—421.   0088

Hibbard, G. R. The Country House Poem of the Seventeenth Century. Journal of the Warburg and Courtauld Institute, 19: 159—174.   0089

Nelson, Lowry, Jr. The Rhetoric of Ineffability: Toward a Definition of Mystical Poetry. Comparative Literature, 8: 323-336.   0090

Read, Herbert. The Nature of Metaphysical Poetry. In The Nature of Literature, pp. 69—88. New York, Horizon [first American edn.].   0091

Tillyard, E. M. W. The Metaphysicals and Milton. London, Chatto and Windus. vii, 87 p.   0092

Tyler, Parker. Phaethon: The Metaphysical Tension between the Ego and the Universe in English Poetry. Accent, 16: 29—44.   0093

GENERAL STUDIES

1957

0094 Kermode, Frank. Dissociation of Sensibility. KR, 19: 169—194.

0095 Langvardt, Arthur LeRoy. The Verse Epigram in England During the Sixteenth and Early Seventeenth Centuries. DA, 17: 2595—2596.

0096 Miles, Josephine. Eras and Modes in English Poetry. Berkeley, University of California. 233 p.

0097 Stickney, Ruth F. Formal Verse Satire from Lodge to Jonson, with Particular Reference to the Imitation of Classical Models. DA, 17: 2017

0098 Swardson, Harold Roland, Jr. A Study of the Tension Between Christian and Classical Traditions in Seventeenth Century Poetry. DA, 17: 1559.

1958

0099 Patrides, C. A. Renaissance and Modern Thought on the Last Things: A Study in Changing Conceptions. Harvard Theological Review, 51: 169—185.

0100 Warnke, Frank J. Jan Luyken: A Dutch Metaphysical Poet. Comparative Literature, 10: 45—54.

0101 Watson, George. Ramus, Miss Tuve and the New Petromachia. MP, 55: 259—262.

0102 Wilson, E. M. Spanish and English Religious Poetry of the Seventeenth Century. Journal of Ecclesiastical History, 9: 38—53.

1959

0103 Attal, Jean-Pierre. Qu'est-ce que la poésie "métaphysique"? Critique (Paris), 15: 682—707.

0104 Cain, Thomas Henry. The Poem of Compliment in the English Renaissance. DA, 20: 2285.

0105 Colie, Rosalie L. Constantijn Huygens and the Metaphysical Mode. Germanic Review, 34: 59—73.

0106 Duncan, Joseph E. The Revival of Metaphysical Poetry. Minneapolis, University of Minnesota. 227 p.

0107 Gamberini, Spartaco. Poeti Metafisici e Cavalieri in Inghilterra. Firenze, L. S. Olschki. 269 p.

10

GENERAL STUDIES

Locke, Julius Duane. Images and Image Symbolism   0108
in Metaphysical Poetry with Special Reference to
Otherworldliness. DA, 19: 1743.

Milch, Werner. Metaphysical Poetry and the Ger-   0109
man "Barocklyrik." Comparative Literature
Studies, 23—24: 16—22.

Richmond, H. M. The Intangible Mistress. MP,   0110
56: 217—223.

1960

Allen, Don Cameron. Image and Meaning. Balti-   0111
more, John Hopkins. viii, 175 p.

Crossett, John. Did Johnson Mean "Paraphysi-   0112
cal"? Boston University Studies in English, 4:
121—124.

Daiches, David. A Critical History of English Lit-   0113
erature. New York, Ronald. 2 v.

Ellrodt, Robert. L'Inspiration personnelle et l'es-   0114
prit due temps chez les poètes métaphysiques
anglais. Annales de L'Université de Paris, 30:
167—169.

Ellrodt, Robert. L'inspiration personnelle et L'es-   0115
prit du temps chez les poètes métaphysiques
anglais. Paris, José Corti. 2 v. in 3.

Iser, Wolfgang. Manieristische Metaphorik in   0116
der englischen Dichtung. Germanisch-Roma-
nische Monatsschrift, neue folge, 10: 266—287.

Muraoka, Isamu. The Historical Background of   0117
Metaphysical Poetry. Studies in English Literature (Tokyo), 36: 49—64.

Wedgwood, C. V. Poetry and Politics Under the   0118
Stuarts. Cambridge, Cambridge University. vii,
219 p.

no date

Gregory, H. (ed). Critical Remarks on the Meta-   0119
physical Poets. Mt. Vernon, Golden Eagle.

THOMAS CAREW

1941

Dunlap, Rhodes.   Thomas Carew, Thomas Carey,   0120
and "The Sovereign of the Seas." MLN, 56:
268—271.

1947

Herrick, Allen.   Thomas Carew. TLS, April 12, p.   0121
171.

1949

Carew, Thomas.   The Poems of Thomas Carew.   0122
Edited by Rhodes Dunlap. Oxford, Clarendon,
lxxx, 297 p.

1950

Maxwell, J. C.   Lucy Ashton's Song. N&Q, 195:   0123
210.

1951

Duncan-Jones, E. E.   Carew and Guez de Balzac.   0124
MLR, 46: 439—440.
Shapiro, I. A.   Carew's "Obsequies to the Lady   0125
Anne Hay." N&Q, 196: 7—8.

1952

Howarth, R. G.   A Poem by Carew? N&Q, 197:   0126
518.

1953

Baker, Donald C.   Carew's "Disdaine Returned."   0127

Explicator, 11: 54.

0128   E., R.   Carew's "Disdain Returned." Explicator, 11:
Q3.

0129   Emslie, Macdonald.   Carew's "Disdaine Returned."
Explicator, 12: 4.

1954

0130   Blanshard, Rufus A.   Thomas Carew and the Cavalier Poets.   Transactions of the Wisconsin Academy, 43: 97—105.

0131   Crum, M. C.   Bibliographical Notes: Notes on the
Texts of William Lawes's Songs in B.M.   MS
Add. 31432.   The Library, 5th ser., 9: 122—127.

0132   Duncan-Jones, E. E.   Carew's "Upon the Kings
Sicknesse."   Explicator, 13: 19.

0133   Grivelet, Michel.   Note sur Thomas Heywood et le
Théâtre sous Charles Ier.   Études Anglaises, 7:
101—106.

1955

0134   Blanshard, Rufus A.   Carew and Jonson.   SP, 52:
195—211.

1956

0135   Biggs, Alan J.   Carew and Shakespeare.   N&Q, N.S.
3: 225.

1957

0136   Blanshard, Rufus A.   Thomas Carew's Master Figures.   Boston University Studies in English, 3:
214—227.

0137   Ruoff, James E.   Thomas Carew's Early Reputation.
N&Q, N.S. 4: 61—62.

1958

0138   Schoff, Francis G.   Thomas Carew: Son of Ben or
Son of Spenser.   Discourse, 1: 8—24.

0139   Selig, Edward I.   The Flourishing Wreath: A Study
of Thomas Carew's Poetry.   New Haven, Yale
University.   ix, 185 p.

JOHN CLEVELAND

1939

Mathieson, J. F.   Cleveland on Tyranny.   N&Q,   0140
177: 136.

1942

Hanson, Laurence.   Points in the Bibliographies of   0141
John Cleveland and Alexander Brome.   RES, 18:
321—322.

1949

Turner, Alberta.   The University Miscellanies: 0142
Some Neglected Early Texts of Cleveland and
Cowley. MLN, 64: 423—424.

1951

Woolf, Henry Bosley.   John Cleveland's "West   0143
Saxon Poet." PQ, 30: 443—447.

1955

Kimmey, John L.   John Cleveland: His Poetry and   0144
Influence. DA, 15: 1388—1389.

1956

Morris, B. R.   John Cleveland. TLS, January 13,   0145
p. 21.

1957

Emslie, Macdonald.   Pepy's Songs and Songbooks   0146
in the Diary Period. The Library, 5th ser., 12:
240—255.

JOHN CLEVELAND

1958

0147   Kimmey, John L.   John Cleveland and the Satiric
        Couplet in the Restoration. PQ, 37: 410—423.
0148   Wedgwood, C. V.   A Metaphysical Satirist. Lis-
        tener, 59: 769—771.

ABRAHAM COWLEY

1939

Vincent, Howard P.   Three Unpublished Letters of   0149
Abraham Cowley.   MLN, 54: 454—458.

1940

Bradner, Leicester.   Musae Anglicanae: A History   0510
of Anglo-Latin Poetry 1500—1925.   New York,
Modern Language Association.   xii, 383 p.
Das, P. K.   Cowley and Wordsworth's "Skylark."   0151
("Ethereal Minstrel").   MLR, 35: 214.
Mead, H. R.   [Variant Issues of Cowley's Verses]   0152
PBSA, 35: 68.

1942

Simmons, J.   An Unpublished Letter from Abraham   0153
Cowley.   MLN, 57: 194—195.

1943

Pettet, E. C.   A Study of Abraham Cowley.   English,   0154
4: 86—89.

1944

H., R.   "Love's Philosophy."   N&Q, 186: 49.   0155

1945

Hussey, Richard.   A Quotation by Byron.   N&Q,   0156
188: 85.
Thorpe, W. A.   A Quotation by Byron.   N&Q, 188:   0157
151.

ABRAHAM COWLEY

1948

0158   Allen, Don Cameron.   Cowley's Pindar.   MLN, 63:
184—185.

0159   Cowley, Abraham.   Essay upon Satyr . . . London . . .
Dring . . . 1680.   Edited by G. R. Noyes and H. R.
Mead.   University of California Publications in
English, 7: 139—155.

0160   Elledge, Scott.   Cowley's Ode "Of Wit" and Longinus
On the Sublime: A Study of One Definition of the
Word Wit.   MLQ, 9: 185—198.

0161   Miller, C. William   Cowley and Evelyn's Kalen-
darium Hortense.   MLN, 63: 398—401.

1949

0162   Cowley, Abraham.   Poetry and Prose.   Introduction
and Notes by L. C. Martin.   Oxford, Clarendon.
xlvii, 128 p.

0163   Kermode, Frank.   The Date of Cowley's Davideis.
RES, 25: 154—158.

0164   Turner, Alberta.   The University Miscellanies:
Some Neglected Early Texts of Cleveland and
Cowley.   MLN, 64: 423—424.

1951

0165   Korn, A. L.   Mac Flecknoe and Cowley's Davideis.
HLQ, 14: 99—127.

0166   Mead, H. R.   Two Issues of Cowley's "Vision."
PBSA, 45: 77—81.

0167   Vieth, D. M.   Rochester and Cowley.   TLS, October
12, p. 645.

1953

0168   Ghosh, J. C.   Abraham Cowley (1618—1667).   SR,
61: 433—447.

0169   Smith, Harold W.   Cowley, Marvell and the Second
Temple.   Scrutiny, 19: 184—205.

1956

0170   Hinman, Robert B.   "Truth is Truest Poesy": The
Influence of the New Philosophy on Abrham Cowley.   ELH, 23: 194—203.

ABRAHAM COWLEY

1957

Arber, Agnes. Dryden and Cowley: "Star-Slime."   0171
TLS, June 7, p. 349.

Brooks, Harold F. Dryden and Cowley. TLS, April   0172
19, p. 245.

Cohane, J. J. Cowley and Yeats. TLS, May 10, p.   0173
289.

Emslie, Macdonald. Pepy's Songs and Songbooks   0174
in the Diary Period. The Library, 5th ser., 12:
240—255.

Nathanson, Leonard. The Context of Dryden's   0175
Criticism of Donne's and Cowley's Love Poetry.
N&Q, N.S. 4: 56—59.

Nathanson, Leonard. Dryden, Donne, and Cowley.   0176
N&Q, N.S. 4: 197—198.

Noll, Lou Barker. The Lyrical Achievement of   0177
Abraham Cowley. DA, 17: 2270—2271.

Scudamore, W. K. Star-Slime. TLS, June 14, p.   0178
365.

1958

Suerbaum, Ulrich. Die Lyrik der Korrespondenzen: 0179
Cowleys Bildkunst und die Tradition der englis-
chen Renaissancedichtung. Bochum-Langendreer,
H. Pöppinghaus. 287 p.

1960

Duncan, Margaret. Cowley's Elegy on John Little-   0180
ton. N&Q, N.S. 7: 426—427.

Hinman, Robert B. Abraham Cowley's World of   0181
Order. Cambridge, Harvard University. vii,
373 p.

RICHARD CRASHAW

Santa Teresa (Estudio y Version). Escorial Revista de Cultura y Letras, 9, No. 26: 447—468.

1944

0191   Bernard, Sister Miriam.   More than a Woman.   Catholic World, 160: 52—57.

0192   Logan, Sister Eugenia.   An Indebtedness of Coleridge to Crashaw.   MLN, 59: 551—553.

1945

0193   Hess, M. Whitcomb.   Descartes and Richard Crashaw.   Commonweal, 42: 455—457.

0194   Moloney, Michael F.   Richard Crashaw.   Catholic World, 162: 43—50.

0195   Praz, Mario.   Richard Crashaw.   Brescia, Morcelliana.   200 p.

1946

0196   Anon.   Poet and Saint.   TLS, June 1, p. 258.

0197   Hess, M. Whitcomb.   Recalling Crashaw.   America, 74: 381—382.

1947

0198   Allison, A. F.   Some Influences in Crashaw's Poem "On a Prayer Booke Sent to Mrs. M. R."   RES, 23: 34—42.

1948

0199   Allison, A. F.   Crashaw and St. François de Sales. RES, 24: 295—302.

0200   Neill, Kerby.   Structure and Symbol in Crashaw's Hymn on the Nativity.   PMLA, 63: 101—113.

0201   Williams, George W.   Crashaw's "Letter to the Countess of Denbigh."   Explicator, 6: 48.

1949

0202   Anon.   A Poet of Delights.   TLS, August 19, p. 536.

0203   Crashaw, Richard.   The Verse in English of Richard Crashaw.   New York, Grove.   255 p.

0204   Meath, Gerard.   The Tumbling Images of Richard Crashaw.   Listener, 42: 366—367.

0205   Moloney, Michael F.   Richard Crashaw: 1649—

RICHARD CRASHAW

1949. Catholic World, 169: 336—340.

Praz, Mario. Drummond and Crashaw. TLS, Octo- 0206
ber 21, p. 681.

Turnell, Martin. Richard Crashaw After Three Hun- 0207
dred Years. Nineteenth Century, 146: 100—114.

Watkin, E. I. William Crashaw's Influence on His 0208
Son. Dublin Review, no. 446, pp. 1-25.

Willey, Basil. Richard Crashaw. Cambridge, Cam- 0209
bridge University. 25 p.

Williams, George W. Textual Revision in Cra- 0210
shaw's "Vpon the Bleeding Crvcifix." SB, 1:
191—193.

1950

Cammell, Charles R. The Divine Poet: Richard 0211
Crashaw. National and English Review, 135:
230—235.

Maxwell, J. C. Steps to the Temple: 1646 and 0212
1648. PQ, 29: 216—220.

1951

Jacquot, Jean. "Le Duel Musical" de Richard 0213
Crashaw et sa Source Italienne. Revue de Littérature Comparée, 25: 232—241.

1952

Martin, L. C. An Unedited Crashaw Manuscript. 0214
TLS, April 18, p. 272.

1953

Peter, John. Crashaw and "The Weeper." Scrutiny, 0215
19: 258—273.

1954

Wallis, P. J. William Crashaw—Puritan Divine, 0216
Poet, and Bibliophile. N&Q, N.S. 1: 101—102.

1955

Adams, Robert M. Taste and Bad Taste in Meta- 0217
physical Poetry: Richard Crashaw and Dylan
Thomas. Hudson Review, 8: 61—77.

Manning, Stephen. The Meaning of "The Weeper." 0218

23

RICHARD CRASHAW

ELH, 22: 34—47.

0219 Rickey, Mary Ellen. Crashaw and Vaughan. N&Q, N.S. 2: 232—233.

0220 Rickey, Mary Ellen. A Study of the Rhymes of the Metaphysical Poets with Particular Reference to Richard Crashaw. DA, 15: 1621—1622.

1956

0221 Collmer, Robert G. Crashaw's "Death More Misticall and High." JEGP, 55: 373—380.

0222 Farnham, Anthony E. Saint Teresa and the Coy Mistress. Boston University Studies in English, 2: 226—239.

0223 Rickey, Mary Ellen. Chapman and Crashaw. N&Q, N.S. 3: 472—473.

0224 Williams, George W. Richard Crashaw and the Little Gidding Bookbinders. N&Q, N.S. 3: 9—10.

1957

0225 Crashaw, Richard. The Poems, English, Latin and Greek, of Richard Crashaw. Edited by L. C. Martin. 2nd edn. Oxford, Clarendon. xciv, 476 p.

0226 Pettoello, Laura. A Current Misconception Concerning the Influence of Marino's Poetry on Crashaw's. MLR, 52: 321—328.

0227 Wallis, P. J. The Library of William Crashawe. Transactions of the Cambridge Bibliographical Society, 2 (pt. 2): 213—228.

1958

0228 Madsen, William G. A Reading of "Musicks Duell," pp. 39—50. Studies in Honor of John Wilcox. Detroit, Wayne State University.

0229 Praz, Mario. The Flaming Heart: Essays on Crashaw, Machiavelli, and Other Studies in the Relations Between Italian and English Literature from Chaucer to T. S. Eliot. New York, Doubleday. 390 p.

0230 Saveson, J. E. Richard Crashaw. TLS, February 28, p. 115.

JOHN DONNE

1939

Anon. John Donne's Disdain. TLS, August 26, p. 0231
  502.
Bell, Charles. Donne's "Farewell to Love." TLS, 0232
  July 1, p. 389.
Bennett, Roger E. John Donne and Everard Gilpin. 0233
  RES, 15: 66—72.
Bowers, Fredson T. An Interpretation of Donne's 0234
  Tenth Elegy. MLN, 54: 280—282.
Coon, Arthur M. "Farewell to Love." TLS, August 0235
  12, p. 479.
Donne, John. Poetry and Prose of John Donne. 0236
  Selected and edited by A. Desmond Hawkins.
  New York, Nelson. v, 479 p.
Hennecke, Hans. John Donne und die metaphy- 0237
  sische Lyrik Englands. Die Literatur, 41: 21—
  24.
Ince, Richard B. Angel From a Cloud. London, 0238
  Massie, ix, 452 p.
Moloney, Michael F. John Donne, the Flight From 0239
  Mediaevalism. University of Illinois, Abstracts
  of Dissertations, Urbana. 6 p.
Moses, W. R. The Metaphysical Conceit in the 0240
  Poems of John Donne. Bulletin of Vanderbilt
  University, Abstracts of Theses, 39: 28—29.
Rugoff, Milton A. Donne's Imagery: A Study in 0241
  Creative Sources. New York, Corporate. 270 p.
Sibley, A. M. A Comparative Study of John Donne 0242
  and T. S. Eliot. University of Oklahoma Bulle-
  tin, Abstract of Theses, p. 116.

0243   Simpson, Evelyn M.   Jonson and Donne: A Problem
in Authorship. RES, 15: 274—282.

0244   Williamson, George.   Donne's "Farewell to Love."
MP, 36: 301—303.

1940

0245   Anon.   A Book from Donne's Library. Bodleian Library Record, 1: 147—148.

0246   Anon.   Desiderata Bodleiana (John Donne). Bodleian Library Record, 1: 205.

0247   Anon.   John Donne Desiderata. Yale University Library Gazette, 15: 47—48.

0248   Bennett, Roger E.   Donne's Letters from the Conti-
nent in 1611—1612. PQ, 19: 66—78.

0249   Brown, Mary.   Verses on Donne's Burial. N&Q,
178: 12.

0250   Combs, Homer Carroll and Zay Rusk Sullens.   A
Concordance to the English Poems of John Donne.
Chicago, Packard. ix, 418 p.

0251   Coon, Arthur M.   Verses on Donne's Burial (clxxviii.
12). N&Q, 178: 251.

0252   Escott, H.   The Modern Relevance of John Donne.
Congregational Quarterly, 28: 57—64.

0253   Evans, B. Ifor.   Tradition and Romanticism: Studies
in English Poetry from Chaucer to W. B. Yeats.
London, Methuen. 213 p.

0254   Hijikata, Tatsuzo.   John Donne's "Songs and
Sonets." Studies in English Literature (Tokyo),
20: 336—347.

0255   M., M.   Satires and Sermons by John Donne. More
Books: Bulletin of the Boston Public Library, 15:
251—252.

0256   Moloney, Michael F.   The End of the Renaissance.
Catholic World, 152: 189—195.

0257   Nicolson, Marjorie H.   Kepler, the Somnium, and
John Donne. JHI, 1: 259—280.

0258   Potter, George R.   Donne's Paradoxes in 1707. MLN,
55: 53.

0259   Van de Water, C.   First of the Moderns. Scholas-
tic, 37 (October 28): 20.

0260   Williamson, George.   Textual Difficulties in the
Interpretation of Donne's Poetry. MP, 38: 37—72.

JOHN DONNE

1941

Allen, Don Cameron. Donne and the Bezoar. MLN, 0261
56: 609—611

Allen, Don Cameron. Donne's Suicides. MLN, 56: 0262
129—133.

Anon. Hemingway's Title. Wilson Library Bulle- 0263
tin, 15: 515.

Anon. John Donne, O.P. Time Magazine, 37 (Jan- 0264
uary 13): 76.

Babb, Lawrence. Melancholy and the Elizabethan 0265
Man of Letters. HLQ, 4: 247—261.

Benham, Allen R. The Myth of John Donne the 0266
Rake, pp. 273—281. Renaissance Studies in
Honor of Hardin Craig. Stanford, Stanford Uni-
versity. Also printed in: PQ, 20: 465—473.

Bennett, Joan. An Aspect of the Evolution of 0267
Seventeenth Century Prose. RES, 17: 281—297.

Bennett, Roger E. Donne's Letters to Severall Per- 0268
sons of Honour. PMLA, 56: 120—140.

Botting, R. B. The Reputation of John Donne Dur- 0269
ing the Nineteenth Century. Research Studies
of the State College of Washington, 9: 139—188.

Carleton, Phillips D. John Donne's "Bracelet of 0270
Bright Hair About the Bone." MLN, 56: 366—
368.

Donne, John. The Complete Poetry and Selected 0271
Prose of John Donne and the Complete Poems of
William Blake. Introduction and Notes by Robert
Hillyer. New York, Random House. lv, 1045.

Donne, John. Ignatius his Conclave. Edited by 0272
Charles M. Coffin (Facsimile Text Society). New
York, Columbia University. xxiii, 143 p.

Donne, John. The Love Poems of John Donne. 0273
London, Chatto and Windus. xliv p.

Donne, John. Some Poems and a Devotion of John 0274
Donne. Norfolk, Conn., New Directions. 32 p.

Donne, John. Tolling Bell: a Devotion. New York, 0275
Overbrook.

Duncan, Edgar H. Alchemy in the Writings of 0276
Chaucer, Jonson and Donne. Bulletin of Vanderbilt University, Abstracts of Theses, 41: 16—17.

JOHN DONNE

0277   Mathews, Ernst G.   Donne's "Little Rag." MLN,
        56: 607—609.
0278   Muñoz Rojas, José A.   Un Libro Español en la Bib-
        lioteca de Donne. Revista de Filologia Española,
        25: 108—111.
0279   Newdigate, B. H.   Donne's "Letters to Several Per-
        sons of Honour." N&Q, 180: 441.
0280   Oake, Roger B.   Diderot and Donne's BIAΘANATOΣ.
        MLN, 56: 114—115.
0281   Simpson, Evelyn M.   The Text of Donne's "Divine
        Poems." Essays and Studies, 26: 88—105.
0282   Simpson, Percy.   King James on Donne. TLS, Octo-
        ber 25, p. 531.
0283   Unger, Leonard H.   Donne's Poetry and Modern
        Definitions of "Metaphysical": A Critical Study.
        University of Iowa Doctoral Dissertations Ab-
        stracts, 4: 221—223.
0284   White, William.   John Donne Since 1900: A Bib-
        liography of Periodical Articles. Bulletin of
        Bibliography, 17: 86—89, 113, 165—171, 192—
        195.

1942

0285   Battenhouse, Roy W.   The Grounds of Religious
        Toleration in the Thought of John Donne. Church
        History, 11: 217—248.
0286   Bennett, Roger E.   John Donne and the Earl of Es-
        sex. MLQ, 3: 603—604.
0287   Cooper, Harold.   John Donne and Virginia in 1610.
        MLN, 57: 661—663.
0288   Donne, John.   The Complete Poems of John Donne.
        Edited by Roger E. Bennett. Chicago, Packard.
        xxix, 306 p.
0289   Duncan, E. H.   Donne's Alchemical Figures. ELH,
        9: 257—285.
0290   Fiedler, L.   John Donne's Songs and Sonets: A
        Reinterpretation in the Light of Their Traditional
        Backgrounds. Summaries of Doctoral Disserta-
        tions, University of Wisconsin, 6: 281—282.
0291   Hardy, Evelyn.   Donne: A Spirit in Conflict. Lon-
        don, Constable. xi, 274 p.
0292   Heywood, Terence.   Some Notes on English Ba-

roque. Horizon, 2: 267—270.

Legouis, Pierre. Some Lexicological Notes and   0293
Queries on Donne's Satires. Studia Neophilo-
logica, 14: 184—196.

McClure, N. E. King James on Bacon. TLS, Jan-   0294
uary 17, p. 31.

Maycock, H. John Donne, Dean of St. Paul's.   0295
Cambridge Review, 63: 164—165.

Milgate, W. Donne the Lawyer. TLS, August 1,   0296
p. 379.

Milgate, W. The Importance of John Donne.   0297
Southerly (Sydney), 2: 33—34.

Richards, I. A. The Interaction of Words. In The   0298
Language of Poetry, pp. 65—87. Edited by Allen
Tate. Princeton, Princeton University.

Simpson, Evelyn M. A Donne Manuscript in St.   0299
Paul's Cathedral Library. PQ, 21: 237—239.

Simpson, Evelyn M. Queries from Donne. N&Q,   0300
182: 64.

Smith, R. G. Augustine and Donne: A Study in   0301
Conversion. Theology, 45: 147—159.

Sommerlatte, K. Churchill and Donne. Saturday   0302
Review of Literature, 25 (December 5): 27.

Stein, Arnold. Donne and the Couplet. PMLA, 57:   0303
676—696.

Titus, O. P. Science and John Donne. Scientific   0304
Monthly, 54: 176—178.

White, William. John Donne Since 1900: A Bibli-   0305
ography of Periodicals. Bulletin of Bibliography
Pamphlets, no. 37. Boston, F. W. Faxon. v, 23.

1943

Allen, Don Cameron. Dean Donne Sets His Text.   0306
ELH, 10: 208—229.

Allen, Don Cameron. John Donne and Pierio Va-   0307
leriano. MLN, 58: 610—612.

Allen, Don Cameron. John Donne's Knowledge of   0308
Renaissance Medicine. JEGP, 42: 322—342.

Arms, George W. Donne's Song, "Go and Catch a   0309
Falling Star." Explicator, 1: 29.

Donne, John. Love Poems of John Donne Together   0310
with the Devotion "For Whom the Bell Tolls."

Mt. Vernon, New York, Peter Pauper. 73 p.

0311 Donne, John. Probleme XI. San Francisco, Pox
Populi.

0312 Duncan, Edgar H. Donne's "A Valediction: Forbidding Mourning." Explicator, 1: 63.

0313 Editors, The. Donne's Song "Go and Catch a Falling
Star." Explicator, 1: 29.

0314 Grierson, H. J. C. A Spirit in Conflict. Spectator,
170: 293.

0315 Kirby, J. P. Donne's Song "Go and Catch a Falling
Star." Explicator, 1: 29.

0316 Locke, L. G. Donne's Song, "Go and Catch a Falling Star." Explicator, 1: 29.

0317 Memorabilist. Some Notes on Donne. N&Q, 184:
77, 165—166.

0318 Mizener, Arthur. Some Notes on the Nature of English Poetry. SR, 51: 27—51.

0319 Simpson, Percy. The Rhyming of Stressed and Un-
stressed Syllables in Elizabethan Verse. MLR,
38: 127—129.

0320 Tillyard, E. M. W. A Note on Donne's Extasie.
RES, 19: 67—70.

0321 Whitesell, J. E. Donne's Song, "Go and Catch a
Falling Star." Explicator, 1: 29.

1944

0322 Campbell, H. M. Donne's "Hymn to God, My God,
in My Sickness." College English, 5: 192—196.

0323 Gardner, Helen. John Donne: A Note on Elegy V,
"His Picture." MLR, 39: 333—337.

0324 Garrod, H. W. The Date of Donne's Birth. TLS,
December 30, p. 636.

0325 Gilpatrick, Naomi. Autobiographies of Grace.
Catholic World, 159: 52—57.

0326 Howarth, R. G. John Donne—Undone. Southerly
(Sydney), 4: 43.

0327 Milgate, W. John Donne—Undone. Southerly (Sydney), 4: 8—11.

0328 Moloney, Michael F. John Donne, His Flight From
Mediaevalism. Urbana, University of Illinois.
223 p.

0329 Simpson, Evelyn M. Notes on Donne. RES, 20:

JOHN DONNE

224—227.

Stein, Arnold.　Donne and the Satiric Spirit.　ELH,　0330
11: 266—282.
Stein, Arnold.　Donne's Harshness and Elizabethan　0331
Tradition.　SP, 41: 390—409.
Stein, Arnold.　Donne's Prosody.　PMLA, 59: 373—　0332
397.
Stein, Arnold.　Meter and Meaning in Donne's　0333
Verse.　SR, 52: 288—301.
Svendsen, Kester.　Donne's "A Hymne to God the　0334
Father."　Explicator, 2: 62.

1945

Allen, Don Cameron.　John Donne's "Paradise and　0335
Calvarie."　MLN, 60: 398—400.
Allen, Don Cameron.　Two Annotations on Donne's　0336
Verse.　MLN, 60: 54—55.
Brooks, Cleanth.　Shakespeare as a Symbolist　0337
Poet.　Yale Review, N.S. 34: 642—665.
Donne, John.　John Donne "Hengivelsen."　Over-　0338
sættelse: Ove Abildgaard; Træsnit: Povl
Christensen.　København, H. Hirschsprungs.
21 p.
Donne, John.　O Pilgrim Soul.　Ó Duše Poutniku.　0339
Thirteen Poems translated into Czech by Libuse
Pánková, with Commentary by Herbert Read.　Lon-
don, English and Czechoslovak P.E.N. Clubs. 32 p.
Garrod, H. W.　Donne and Mrs. Herbert.　RES, 21:　0340
161—173.
Garrod, H. W.　The Latin Poem Addressed by　0341
Donne to Dr. Andrews.　RES, 21: 38—42.
Mabbott, Thomas O.　John Donne and Valeriano.　0342
MLN, 60: 358.
Memorabilist.　Sir Richard Baker on John Donne.　0343
N&Q, 188: 257.
Miles, Josephine.　From "Good" to "Bright": A　0344
Note in Poetic History.　PMLA, 60: 766—774.
Potter, George R.　Hitherto Undescribed Manu-　0345
script Versions of Three Sermons by Donne.
JEGP, 44: 28—35.
Praz, Mario.　La Poesia Metafisica Inglese del　0346
Seicento.　John Donne.　Roma, Edizioni italiani.
173 p.

JOHN DONNE

0347   Raine, K.   John Donne and the Baroque Doubt.
       Horizon, 11: 371—395.
0348   Umbach, Herbert H.   The Merit of Metaphysical
       Style in Donne's Easter Sermons. ELH, 12: 108—
       129.
0349   Wiggins, Elizabeth Lewis.   Logic in the Poetry of
       John Donne. SP, 42: 41—60.

1946

0350   Allen, Don Cameron.   Donne Among the Giants.
       MLN, 61: 257—260.
0351   Allen, Don Cameron.   Donne, Butler, and ?   MLN,
       61: 65.
0352   Allen, Don Cameron.   Donne's Specular Stone.
       MLN, 61: 63—64.
0353   Donne, John.   John Donne Poems (1633).   Paris,
       Société d'Édition "Les Belles Lettres."   60 p.
0354   Donne, John.   John Donne Poetry and Prose.   Edited
       by H. W. Garrod. (Clarendon English Series).
       Oxford, Clarendon. lviii, 126 p.
0355   Donne, John.   Poetry and Prose of John Donne.
       Selected by Walter S. Scott. London, Westhouse.
       444 p.
0356   Donne, John.   A Sermon Preached at Lincoln's Inn
       by John Donne. Edited by George Potter. Stan-
       ford, Stanford University. vii, 71 p.
0357   Donne, John.   Sermoni. Translated di Margherti
       Guidacci della scelta di L. P. Smith. Firenzi,
       Liberia Editrice Fiorentina.
0358   Dunlap, Rhodes.   Donne as Navigator. TLS, Decem-
       ber 28, p. 643.
0359   Everson, W.   Donne's "The Apparition."   Explicator,
       4: 56.
0360   Gardner, Helen.   Notes on Donne's Verse Letters.
       MLR, 41: 318—321.
0361   Gilbert, Allan H.   Donne's "The Apparition."   Ex-
       plicator, 4: 56.
0362   Grierson, H. J. C.   John Donne. TLS, July 20, p.
       343.
0363   Jones, H. W.   John Donne. TLS, July 20, p. 343.
0364   Lederer, Josef.   John Donne and the Emblematic
       Practice. RES, 22: 182—200.

JOHN DONNE

Milgate, W.   The Date of Donne's Birth. N&Q,   0365
191: 206—208.

Milgate, W.   A Note on Donne. Southerly (Syd-   0366
ney), 6: 120—121.

Miller, C. William.   Donne's "The Apparition."   0367
Explicator, 4: 24.

Minton, A.   Donne's "The Perfume." Explicator,   0368
4: 50.

Norton, Dan S.   Donne's "The Apparition." Expli- 0369
cator, 4: 24.

Perry, H. T. E.   Donne's "The Perfume." Expli-   0370
cator, 5: 10.

Praz, Mario.   Studi sul Concettismo: John Donne.   0371
Firenze, G.C. Sansoni. vii, 321 p.

Simpson, Evelyn M.   The Date of Donne's "Hymne   0372
to God my God, in my Sicknesse." MLR, 41:
9—15.

Sparrow, John.   Donne's "Anniversaries." TLS,   0373
June 29, p. 312.

Sparrow, John.   A Motto of John Donne. TLS,   0374
March 30, p. 151.

Stein, Arnold.   Donne's Obscurity and the Eliza-   0375
bethan Tradition. ELH, 13: 98—118.

Vallette, Jacques.   Un Précurseur anglais des   0376
poètes contemporains. Le Monde, June 20, p. 3.

1947

Allen, Don Cameron.   Donne's Phoenix. MLN, 62:   0377
340—342.

Bourne, Raymund.   John Donne and the Spiritual   0378
Life. Poetry Review, 38: 460—461.

Brooks, Cleanth.   The Well Wrought Urn: Studies   0379
in the Structure of Poetry. New York. Reynal
and Hitchcock. xi, 270 p.

Donne, John.   A Prayer by John Donne. New York,   0380
Banyan. 6 p.

Fausset, Hugh I'Anson.   Poets and Pundits. Lon-   0381
don, Jonathan Cape. 319 p.

Gegenheimer, A. F.   They Might Have Been Ameri-   0382
cans. South Atlantic Quarterly, 46: 511—523.

Hayward, John.   The Nonesuch Donne. TLS, July   0383
5, p. 337.

JOHN DONNE

0384   Hickey, Robert L.   Donne and Virginia.   PQ, 26:
        181—192.
0385   Howell, A. C.   John Donne's Message for the Con-
        temporary Preacher.   Religion in Life, 16: 216—
        233.
0386   Johnson, Stanley F.   John Donne and the Virginia
        Company.   ELH, 14: 127—138.
0387   Keister, Don A.   Donne and Herbert of Cherbury:
        An Exchange of Verses.   MLQ, 8: 430—434.
0388   Martz, Louis L.   John Donne in Meditation: The
        Anniversaries.   ELH, 14: 247—273.
0389   Moloney, Michael F.   John Donne and the Jesuits.
        MLQ, 8: 426—429.
0390   Neill, Kerby.   Donne's "Aire and Angels."   Expli-
        cator, 6: 8.
0391   Roberts, Donald R.   The Death Wish of John Donne.
        PMLA, 62: 958—976.
0392   Roth, R.   Donne and Sonnets IX and X.   Gifthorse,
        1946—1947, pp. 15—18.
0393   Simpson, Evelyn M.   Donne's Sermons.   TLS, March
        15, p. 115.
0394   Stephens, James.   The Prince of Wits.   Listener,
        37: 149—150.
0395   Wagner, G. A.   John Donne and the Spiritual Life.
        Poetry Review, 38: 253—258.

1948

0396   Allen, Don Cameron.   Style and Certitide.   ELH, 15:
        167—175.
0397   Bald, R. C.   A Spanish Book of Donne's.   N&Q, 193:
        302.
0398   Bald, R. C.   William Milbourne, Donne and Thomas
        Jackson.   RES, 24: 321—323.
0399   Christensen, G. J.   Donne's "The Sunne Rising."
        Explicator, 7: 3.
0400   Donne, John.   The Love Poems of Robert Herrick
        and John Donne.   Edited by Louis Untermeyer.
        New Brunswick, Rutgers University.   xv, 251 p.
0401   Dunlap, Rhodes.   The Date of Donne's "The Annun-
        ciation and Passion."   MLN, 63: 258—259.
0402   Gardner, Helen.   John Donne.   British Africa Monthly,
        1(15): 31—32.

JOHN DONNE

Gierasch, W. Donne's "The Sunne Rising." Expli- 0403
cator, 6: 47.

Grierson, H. J. C. John Donne and the "Via Media." 0404
MLR, 43: 305—314.

Howarth, R. G. John Donne, an Evicted Minister. 0405
N&Q, 193: 41.

Huntley, F. L. Donne's "Aire and Angels." Expli- 0406
cator, 6: 53.

Husain, Itrat. John Donne's Seals. N&Q, 193: 0407
567.

Johnson, Stanley F. Sir Henry Goodere and Donne's 0408
Letters. MLN, 63: 38—43.

Maxwell, J. C. A Note on Donne. N&Q, 193: 4. 0409

Nance, John. John Donne and the Spiritual Life. 0410
Poetry Review, 39: 91—92.

Simpson, Evelyn M. Donne's Spanish Authors. 0411
MLR, 43: 182—185.

Simpson, Evelyn M. A Study of the Prose Works 0412
of John Donne. 2nd edn. Oxford, Clarendon.
vii, 371 p.

Ure, Peter. "The Deformed Mistress" Theme and 0413
the Platonic Convention. N&Q, 193: 269—270.

Ward, E. "Death be Not Proud. . . ." English "A" 0414
Analyst, 12: 1—4.

Wendell, John P. Two Cruxes in the Poetry of 0415
Donne. MLN, 63: 477—481.

Williams, Arnold. The Common Expositor: An 0416
Account of the Commentaries on Genesis, 1527—
1633. Chapel Hill, University of North Carolina.
ix, 297 p.

1949

Allen, Don Cameron. John Donne and the Tower of 0417
Babel. MLN, 64: 481—483.

Allen, Don Cameron. The Legend of Noah: Renais- 0418
sance Rationalism in Art, Science, and Letters.
Urbana, University of Illinois. vii, 221.

Bald, R. C. Donne's Activities. TLS, May 13, p. 0419
313.

Bald, R. C. Donne's Travels. SCN, 7: 1. 0420

Birrell, T. A. Donne's Letters. TLS, November 4, 0421
p. 715.

JOHN DONNE

0422   Cleveland, Edward D.   Donne's "The Primrose."
Explicator, 8: 4.

0423   Danby, John F.   The Poets on Fortune's Hill: Literature and Society, 1580—1610. Cambridge
Journal, 2: 195—211.

0424   Ellrodt, Robert.   An Earlier Version (1619) of William
Drummond's Cypresse Grove. English, 7: 228—
231.

0425   Empson, William.   Donne and the Rhetorical Tradition. KR, 11: 571—587.

0426   Gardner, Helen.   A Crux in Donne. TLS, June 10,
p. 381.

0427   Hamilton, G. Rostrevor.   The Tell-Tale Article: A
Critical Approach to Modern Poetry. London,
Heinemann. xii, 114 p.

0428   Henderson, Hanford.   Donne's "The Will." Explicator, 7: 57.

0429   Hohoff, Curt.   John Donne. Hochland, 41: 138—
147.

0430   Hotson, Leslie.   A Crux in Donne. TLS, April 16,
p. 249.

0431   Keynes, Geoffrey.   Books from Donne's Library.
Transactions of the Cambridge Bibliographical
Society, 1 (pt. 1): 64—68.

0432   Matsuura, Kaichi.   A Study of Donne's Imagery.
Studies in English Literature (Tokyo), 26: 125—
184.

0433   Maxwell, J. C.   A Crux in Donne. TLS, May 6, p.
297.

0434   Milgate, W.   Dr. Donne's Art Gallery. N&Q, 194:
318—319.

0435   Murray, W. A.   Donne and Paracelsus: An Essay
in Interpretation. RES, 25: 115—123.

0436   Pafford, J. H. P.   John Donne's Library. TLS, September 2, p. 569.

0437   Potts, L. J.   Ben Jonson and the Seventeenth Century. English Studies, N.S. 2: 7—24.

0438   Powell, A. C.   John Donne's Library. TLS, September 23, p. 617.

0439   Scott, Walter S.   John Donne and Bermuda. Bermuda Historical Quarterly, 6: 77—78.

0440   Shapiro, I. A.   The Date of Donne's Poem "To Mr.

JOHN DONNE

George Herbert." N&Q, 194: 473—474.

Shapiro, I. A.   Donne's Letters. TLS, October 21,   0441
p. 681.

Shapiro, I. A.   Two Donne Poems. TLS, April 9,   0442
p. 233.

Siegel, Paul N.   Donne's Paradoxes and Problems.   0443
PQ, 28: 507—511.

Sparrow, John.   Two Epitaphs by John Donne. TLS,   0444
March 26, p. 208.

Spitzer, Leo.   A Method of Interpreting Literature.   0445
Northampton, Smith College. 149 p.

Spörri-Sigel, Erika.   Liebe und Tod in John Donnes   0446
Dichtung. Siebnen, Gebr. Kurzi. 98 p.

Thomson, Patricia.   John Donne and the Countess   0447
of Bedford. MLR, 44: 329—340.

Wallerstein, Ruth.   Rhetoric in the English Renais-   0448
sance: Two Elegies, pp. 153—178. English Institute Essays. New York, Columbia University.

Winters, Yvor.   The Poetry of Gerard Manley Hop-   0449
kins. Hudson Review, 1: 455—476; 2: 61—93.

1950

Allen, Don Cameron.   Three Notes on Donne's Po-   0450
etry With a Side Glance at Othello. MLN, 65:
102—106.

Anon.   Poets and Editors. TLS, September 22, p.   0451
597.

Ball, Lee, Jr.   Donne's "The Computation." Ex-   0452
plicator, 8: 44.

Bredvold, Louis I.   The Rise of English Classi-   0453
cism: A Study in Methodology. Comparative
Literature, 2: 253—268.

Donne, John.   John Donne: A Selection of His Po-   0454
etry. Edited by John Hayward. Harmondsworth,
Penguin Books. 182 p.

Faerber, Hansruedi.   Das Paradoxe in der Dichtung   0455
von John Donne. Zürich, A. G. Rüschlikon. 84 p.

Gierasch, W.   Donne's "Negative Love." Expli-   0456
cator, 9: 13.

Gleckner, Robert F. and Gerald Smith.   Donne's   0457
"Love Usury." Explicator, 8: 43.

Keast, William R.   Killigrew's Use of Donne in   0458

JOHN DONNE

"The Parson's Wedding." MLR, 45: 512—515.
0459 Keister, Don A. Donne's "The Will," 40—41. Explicator, 8: 55.
0460 Lees, F. N. References to Donne. N&Q, 195: 482.
0461 Leishman, J. B. Was John Donne a Metaphysician? Listener, 43: 747—748.
0462 Louthan, Doniphan. The Tome-Tomb Pun in Renaissance England. PQ, 29: 375—380.
0463 Mabbott, Thomas O. Donne's "The Will," 40—41. Explicator, 8: 30.
0464 Mathew, David. Sir Tobie Mathew. London, Parrish. 87 p.
0465 Milgate, W. The Early References to John Donne. N&Q, 195: 229—231, 246—247, 290—292, 381—383.
0466 Moloney, Michael F. Donne's Metrical Practice. PMLA, 65: 232—239.
0467 Ochojski, P. M. Did John Donne Repent his Apostasy? American Benedictine Review, 1: 535—548.
0468 Shapiro, I. A. The "Mermaid Club." MLR, 45: 6—17.
0469 Smith, G. Donne's "Love's Usury." Explicator, 8: 43.
0470 Sprott, S. Ernest. The Legend of Jack Donne the Libertine. UTQ, 19: 335—353.
0471 Symes, Gordon. The Paradoxes of Poetry. English, 8: 69—73.
0472 Turnell, Martin. John Donne and the Quest for Unity. Nineteenth Century, 147: 262—274.
0473 Unger, Leonard H. Donne's Poetry and Modern Criticism. Chicago, Regnery. xii, 91 p.
0474 West, Bill C. Anti-Petrarchism: A Study of the Reaction Against the Courtly Tradition in English Love-Poetry from Wyatt to Donne. Summaries of Doctoral Dissertations, Northwestern University, 18: 35—37.
0475 Wilcox, John. Informal Publication of Late Sixteenth-Century Verse Satire. HLQ, 13: 191—200.
0476 Wiley, Margaret L. John Donne and the Poetry of Scepticism. Hibbert Journal, 48: 163—172.

JOHN DONNE

1951

Atkinson, A. D.　Donne Quotations in Johnson's　0477
Dictionary.　N&Q, 196: 387—388.

Bachrach, A. G. H.　Sir Constantyn Huygens and　0478
Ben Jonson.　Neophilologus (Groningen), 35:
120—129.

Brooks, Cleanth.　Milton and the New Criticism.　0479
SR, 59: 1—22.

Donne, John.　An Anatomy of the World. (Fac-　0480
simile of the 1st edition, 1611).　Postscript by
Geoffrey Keynes.　Cambridge, For the Roxburghe
Club.

Donne, John.　John Donne Love Poems Including　0481
"Songs and Sonets" and "Elegies."　Mt. Vernon,
New York, Peter Pauper.　93 p.

Donne, John.　The Prayers of John Donne.　Selected　0482
and edited by Herbert H. Umbach.　New York,
Bookman Associates.　109 p.

Harding, D. W.　Coherence of Theme in Donne's　0483
Poetry.　KR, 13: 427—444.

Ing, Catherine.　Elizabethan Lyrics.　London,　0484
Chatto and Windus.　252 p.

Jack, Ian.　Pope and "the Weighty Bullion of Dr.　0485
Donne's Satires."　PMLA, 66: 1009—1022.

Legouis, Pierre.　Le Thème du Rêve Dans le "Cli-　0486
tandre" de Pierre Corneille, et "The Dreame" de
Donne.　Revue d'Histoire du Théâtre, 3: 164—166.

Leishman, J. B.　The Monarch of Wit: An Analyti-　0487
cal and Comparative Study of the Poetry of John
Donne.　London, Hutchinson.　278 p.

Louthan, Doniphan.　The Poetry of John Donne.　0488
New York, Bookman Associates.　193 p.

Mabbott, Thomas O.　Forms, Moods, Shapes of　0489
Grief.　SCN, 9: 2.

Main, W. W.　Donne's Elegie XIX, "Going to Bed."　0490
Explicator, 10: 14.

Maxwell, J. C.　Donne and the "New Philosophy."　0491
Durham University Journal, 12: 61—64.

Miles, Josephine.　The Language of the Donne　0492
Tradition.　KR, 13: 37—49.

Praz, Mario.　The Critical Importance of the Re-　0493

vived Interest in Seventeenth-Century Metaphysical Poetry. In English Studies Today, pp.
158—166. London, Oxford University.

0494   Simpson, Evelyn M. The Biographical Value of
Donne's Sermons. RES, N.S. 2: 339—357.

0495   Stein, Arnold. Structures of Sound in Donne's
Verse. KR, 13: 20—36, 256—278.

0496   White, Helen C. John Donne and the Psychology
of Spiritual Effort. In The Seventeenth Century;
studies in the history of English Thought and Literature from Bacon to Pope, pp. 355—368. Stanford, Stanford University.

0497   White, Helen C. John Donne in the Twentieth Century. SCN, 9: 2.

1952

0498   Allen, Don Cameron. The Double Journey of John
Donne. In A Tribute to George Coffin Taylor, pp.
83—99. Chapel Hill, University of North Carolina.

0499   Bald, R. C. Donne's Early Verse Letters. HLQ, 15:
283—289.

0500   Bald, R. C. Donne's Letters. TLS, October 24, p.
700.

0501   Bald, R. C. Donne's Letters. TLS, December 19,
p. 837.

0502   Baruch, F. R. Donne and Herbert. TLS, May 30, p.
361.

0503   Bewley, Marius. Religious Cynicism in Donne's
Poetry. KR, 14: 619—646.

0504   Donne, John. Complete Poetry and Selected Prose
of John Donne. Edited by Charles M. Coffin.
New York, Random House. xliii, 594 p.

0505   Donne, John. "La Corona"—Seven Sonnets by John
Donne Set for Mixed Chorus Acapella by A. Didier
Graeffe. SCN, 10: no. 1 (Supplement).

0506   Donne, John. The Divine Poems. Edited by Helen
Gardner. Oxford, Clarendon. xcviii, 147 p.

0507   Donne, John. Essays in Divinity. Edited by Evelyn M. Simpson. Oxford, Clarendon. xxix, 137 p.

0508   Donne, John. John Donne. Selected Poems. Edited
by James Reeves. London, Heinemann. xviii, 104 p

JOHN DONNE

Eldredge, Frances. Further Allusions and Debts   0509
to John Donne. ELH, 19: 214—228.

Frye, Roland M.   John Donne, Junior, on "Biatha-   0510
natos": A Presentation Letter. N&Q, 197: 495—
496.

Jacobsen, Eric.   The Fable is Inverted, or Donne's   0511
Aesop. Classica et Mediaevalia, 13: 1—37.

Legouis, Pierre. L'État présent des controverses   0512
sur la Poésie de Donne. Études Anglaises, 5:
97—106.

Legouis, Pierre.   Le Thème du Rêve Dans le "Cli-   0513
tandre" de Pierre Corneille, et "The Dreame" de
Donne. Revue d'Histoire du Théâtre, 4: 377—378.

Leishman, J. B.   Donne and Herbert. TLS, June 13,   0514
p. 391.

Novarr, David.   Donne's Letters. TLS, October 24,   0515
p. 700.

Potter, George R.   Donne's Development in Pulpit   0516
Oratory. SCN, 10: 13.

Shapiro, I. A.   The Burley Letters. TLS, Septem-   0517
ber 12, p. 597; September 26, p. 629.

Shapiro, I. A.   Donne's Birthdate. N&Q, 197:   0518
310—313.

Siegel, Paul N.   Donne's Cynical Love Poems and   0519
Spenserian Idealism. SCN, 10: 12.

Simon, Irène.   Some Problems of Donne Criticism.   0520
Revue des Langues Vivantes (Bruxelles), 18:
317—324, 393—414.

Skinner, M.   John Donne Not in Germany in 1602.   0521
N&Q, 197: 134.

Smith, Harold W.   "The Dissociation of Sensi-   0522
bility." Scrutiny, 18: 175—188.

Sorrenson, F. S.   The Nature of the Cursus Pattern   0523
in English Oratorical Prose as Studied in Forty-
three Cadences of John Donne and the Collects.
DA, 12: 636—637.

Thomson, Patricia.   The Literature of Patronage,   0524
1580—1630. EIC, 2: 267—284.

Turnell, Martin.   John Donne's Quest for Unity.   0525
Commonweal, 57: 15—18.

Whitlock, Baird W.   The Burley Letters. TLS,   0526
September 19, p. 613.

JOHN DONNE

0527 Whitlock, Baird W. Donne's "First Letter." TLS, August 22, p. 556.
0528 Whitlock, Baird W. Donne's Letters. TLS, October 3, p. 645.

1953

0529 Allen, Don Cameron. A Note on Donne's "Elegy VIII." MLN, 68: 238—239.
0530 Brown, Nancy P. A Note on the Imagery of Donne's "Loves Growth." MLR, 48: 324—327.
0531 Collins, Carvel. Donne's "The Canonization." Explicator, 12: 3.
0532 Donne, John. John Donne. Divine Poems, Devotions, Prayers. Mt. Vernon, New York, Peter Pauper. 115 p.
0533 Donne, John. Poemas de John Donne. Versiones de William Shand y Alberto Girri. Buenos Aires, Botella al Mar. 55 p.
0534 Donne, John. The Sermons of John Donne. Edited by George R. Potter and Evelyn M. Simpson. 10 vols. Berkeley, University of California, 1953— 1962.
0535 Duncan, Joseph E. The Intellectual Kinship of John Donne and Robert Browning. SP, 50: 81—100.
0536 Emslie, Macdonald. A Donne Setting. N&Q, 198: 495.
0537 García Lorca, José. Un aspecto de John Donne: su originalidad. Insula, 86 (Supplemento): 3.
0538 Gardner, Helen. Donne's "Divine Poems." TLS, January 30, p. 73.
0539 Gardner, Helen. None Other Name. Sobernost, 3: 7—12.
0540 Garvin, Katharine. Looking Babies. TLS, November 23, p. 770.
0541 Herman, George. Donne's "Holy Sonnets," XIV. Explicator, 12: 18.
0542 Hunter, G. K. The Dramatic Technique of Shakespeare's Sonnets. EIC, 3: 152—164.
0543 Husain, Itrat. Donne's "Pseudo-Martyr." TLS, June 12, p. 381.
0544 Hynes, Sam L. A Note on Donne and Aquinas. MLR, 48: 179—181.

JOHN DONNE

Johnson, Stanley F. Donne's "Satires," I. Expli- 0545
cator, 11: 53.

Levenson, J. C. "Holy Sonnets," XIV. Explicator, 0546
11: 31.

Lowe, Robert L. Browning and Donne. N&Q, 198: 0547
491—492.

Matsuura, Kaichi. A Study of Donne's Imagery. 0548
Tokyo, Kenkyusha. xiii, 157 p.

Milgate, W. References to John Donne. N&Q, 0549
198: 421—424.

Moran, Berna. Some Notes on Donne's Attitude to 0550
the Problem of Body and Soul. Ingiliz Filolojisi
Dergisi, 3: 69—76.

Morris, David. The Poetry of Gerard Manley Hop- 0551
kins and T. S. Eliot in the Light of the Donne
Tradition: A Comparative Study. Bern, Francke.
144 p.

Potter, George R. and John Butt. Editing Donne 0552
and Pope. Los Angeles, William Andrews Clark
Memorial Library. 23 p.

Saunders, J. W. Donne and Daniel. EIC, 3: 109— 0553
114.

Simon, Irène. Some Problems of Donne Criticism. 0554
Revue des Langues Vivantes, 19: 14—39, 114—
132, 201—202.

Simon, Irène. Some Problems of Donne Criticism. 0555
Brussels, Marcel Didier. 76 p.

Southwell, Robert. An Humble Supplication to Her 0556
Maiestie by Robert Southwell. Edited by R. C.
Bald. Cambridge, Cambridge University. xxii,
79 p.

Sparrow, John. More Donne. TLS, March 13, p. 0557
169.

Sultan, Stanley. Donne's "Satires," I. Explica- 0558
tor, 11: Q6.

Tate, Allen. The Point of Dying: Donne's "Vir- 0559
tuous Men." SR, 61: 76—81.

Whitlock, Baird W. "Cabal" in Donne's Sermons. 0560
N&Q, 198: 153.

Wright, Herbert G. Some Sixteenth and Seven- 0561
teenth Century Writers on the Plague. Essays
and Studies, N.S. 6: 41—55.

1954

0562   Adams, Robert M.   Donne and Eliot: Metaphysicals.
       KR, 16: 278—291.

0563   Allen, Don Cameron.   Donne's "The Will." MLN,
       69: 559—560.

0564   Bennett, J. A. W.   A Note on Donne's "Crosse."
       RES, N.S. 5: 168—169.

0565   Bryan, R. A.   A Sidelight on Donne's Seventeenth
       Century Literary Reputation. South Atlantic Bulle-
       tin, 19 (No. 3): 11.

0566   Bunton, Norma D.   A Rhetorical Analysis of Repre-
       sentative Sermons of John Donne. DA, 14: 1841—
       1842.

0567   Butor, Michael.   Sur "Le Progrès de l'Âme" de John
       Donne. Cahiers du Sud, 38: 276—283.

0568   Coffin, Charles M.   Donne's Divinity. KR, 16: 292—
       298.

0569   Drinkwater, D. J.   More References to John Donne.
       N&Q, N.S. 1: 514—515.

0570   Gindin, J. J.   Renaissance and Modern Theories of
       Irony: Their Application to Donne's Songs and
       Sonets. DA, 14: 2066—2067.

0571   Gransden, K. W.   John Donne. (Men and Books
       Series). London, Longmans, Green. 197 p.

0572   Hunt, Clay.   Donne's Poetry: Essays in Literary
       Analysis. New Haven, Yale University. 256 p.

0573   Kermode, Frank.   Donne Allusions in Howell's
       Familiar Letters. N&Q, N.S. 1: 337.

0574   Keynes, Geoffrey.   John Donne's Sermons. TLS,
       May 28, p. 351.

0575   Kuhlmann, Helene.   John Donne, Betrachtungen
       über Elend und Grösse der Menschen. Die Neu-
       eren Sprachen, N.S. 3: 452—458.

0576   Levenson, J. C.   Donne's "Holy Sonnets," XIV.
       Explicator, 12: 36.

0577   McCann, Eleanor M.   Donne and St. Teresa on the
       "Ecstasy." HLQ, 17: 125—132.

0578   Potter, George R.   John Donne: Poet to Priest, pp.
       105—126. Five Gayley Lectures. Berkeley,
       University of California.

0579   Sawin, Lewis.   The Earliest Use of "Autumnal."

JOHN DONNE

MLN, 69: 558—559.

Sharp, Robert L.   Donne's "Good-morrow" and Cor-   0580
diform Maps.   MLN, 69: 493—495.

Stevenson, David L.   Among His Private Friends,   0581
John Donne?   SCN, 12: 7.

Umbach, Herbert H.   When a Poet Prays.   Cresset,   0582
17: 15—23.

Wallerstein, Ruth.   Sir John Beaumont's Crowne of   0583
Thornes, a Report.   JEGP, 53: 410—434.

Warren, Austin.   The Very Reverend Dr. Donne.   KR,   0584
16: 268—277.

Whitlock, Baird W.   The Dean and the Yeoman.   0585
N&Q, N.S. 1: 374—375.

Whitlock, Baird W.   John Syminges, A Poet's Step-   0586
Father.   N&Q, N.S. 1: 421—424, 465—467.

Wiley, Margaret L.   The Poetry of Donne: Its In-   0587
terest and Influence Today.   Essays and Studies,
N.S. 7: 78—104.

1955

Coleridge, Samuel T.   Coleridge on the Seven-   0588
teenth Century.   Edited by Roberta F. Brinkley.
Durham, Duke University.   xxxviii, 704 p.

Davenport, A.   An Early Reference to John Donne.   0589
N&Q, N.S. 2: 12.

Donne, John.   Poèmes Choisis.   Tr., intro., et   0590
notes, Pierre Legouis.   (Collection bilingue des
Classiques Étrangers).   Paris, Ambier.   224 p.

Elmen, Paul.   John Donne's Dark Lantern.   PSBA,   0591
49: 181—186.

Emslie, Macdonald.   Barclay Squire and Grier-   0592
son's Donne.   N&Q, N.S. 2: 12—13.

Evans, Maurice.   English Poetry in the Sixteenth   0593
Century.   London, Hutchinson.   184 p.

Francis, W. Nelson.   Donne's "Goodfriday 1613.   0594
Riding Westward."   Explicator, 13: 21.

Grenander, M. E.   Donne's "Holy Sonnets," XII.   0595
Explicator, 13: 42.

Malloch, A. E.   Donne's Pseudo-Martyr and   0596
Catalogus Librorum Aulicorum.   MLN, 70: 174—
175.

0597   Novak, Max.   An Unrecorded Reference in a Poem
       by Donne. N&Q, N.S. 2: 471—472.
0598   Sawin, Lewis.   Donne's "The Canonization," 7.
       Explicator, 13: 31.
0599   Sleight, Richard.   John Donne: "A Nocturnall upon
       S. Lucies Day, Being the Shortest Day." In In-
       terpretations, pp. 31—58. London, Routledge
       and Kegan Paul.
0600   Sorlien, R. P., ed.   John Donne and the Christian
       Life: An Anthology of Selected Sermons Preached
       by Donne. With Introductions and Critical and
       Textual Notes. DA, 15: 1391.
0601   Sparrow, John.   Donne's Books in the Middle Temple.
       TLS, July 29, p. 436; August 5, p. 451.
0602   Wendell, John P.   The Poems and Sermons of John
       Donne: A Study of the Parallels and Relation-
       ship Between the Two Forms of Donne's Art. DA,
       15: 595.
0603   Whitlock, Baird W.   "Y^e Curioust Schooler in
       Christendom." RES, N.S. 6: 365—371.
0604   Whitlock, Baird W.   Donne at St. Dunstan's. TLS,
       September 16, p. 548; September 23, p. 564.
0605   Whitlock, Baird W.   The Orphanage Accounts of
       John Donne, Ironmonger. The Guildhall Mis-
       cellany, 4: 22—29.

                           1956

0606   Allen, Don Cameron.   Donne's Compass Figure.
       MLN, 71: 256—257.
0607   Chatman, Seymour.   Mr. Stein on Donne. KR, 18:
       443—451
0608   Cobb, Lucille S.   Donne's "Satyre" II, 49—57. Ex-
       plicator, 15: 8.
0609   Cobb, Lucille S.   Donne's "Satyre" II, 71—72. Ex-
       plicator, 14: 40.
0610   Cross, K. Gustav.   "Balm" in Donne and Shake-
       speare: Ironic Intention in The Extasie. MLN,
       71: 480—482.
0611   Donne, John.   The Songs and Sonets of John Donne.
       Edited by Theodore Redpath. London, Methuen.
       li, 155 p.
0612   Gale, Robert.   Donne's "The Sunne Rising," 27—

30. Explicator, 15: 14.

Gardner, Helen. Donne and the Church. TLS, May 25, p. 320.   0613

Gardner, Helen. The Limits of Literary Criticism. London, Oxford University. 63 p.   0614

Gardner, Helen and J. B. Leishman. Poetic Tradition in Donne. TLS, May 11, p. 283.   0615

Goldberg, M. A. Donne's "A Lecture Upon the Shadow." Explicator, 14: 50.   0616

Grundy, Joan. Donne's Poetry. TLS, April 27, p. 253.   0617

Herman, George. Donne's "Goodfriday, 1613. Riding Westward." Explicator, 14: 60.   0618

Hickey, Robert L. Donne's Art of Preaching. Tennessee Studies in Literature, 1: 65—74.   0619

Hindle, C. J. A Poem by Donne. TLS, June 8, p. 345.   0620

Knox, George. Donne's "Holy Sonnets," XIV. Explicator, 15: 2.   0621

Malloch, A. E. The Techniques and Function of the Renaissance Paradox. SP, 53: 191—203.   0622

Maud, Ralph. Donne's First Anniversary. Boston University Studies in English, 2: 218—225.   0623

Miller, Henry K. The Paradoxical Encomium with Special Reference to Its Vogue in England, 1600—1800. MP, 53: 145—178.   0624

Novarr, David. Donne's "Epithalamion Made at Lincoln's Inn": Context and Date. RES, N.S. 7; 250—263.   0625

Ornstein, Robert. Donne, Montaigne, and Natural Law. JEGP, 55: 213—229.   0626

Rooney, William J. "The Canonization"—the Language of Paradox Reconsidered. ELH, 23: 36—47.   0627

Simpson, Evelyn M. Donne and the Church. TLS, May 25, p. 320.   0628

Smith, A. J. Two Notes on Donne. MLR, 51: 405—407.   0629

Sparrow, John. The Text of Donne. TLS, December 21, p. 765.   0630

Stein, Arnold. Donne's Prosody. KR, 18: 439—443.   0631

Walsh, James E. A Poem by Donne. TLS, April 6, p. 207.   0632

JOHN DONNE

1957

0633   Alvarez, A.   John Donne and His Circle.   Listener, 57: 827—828.

0634   Bradbrook, F. W.   John Donne and Ben Jonson. N&Q, N.S. 4: 146—147.

0635   Camden, Carroll.   Spenser's "Little Fish that Men Call Remora."   Rice Institute Pamphlet, 44: 1—12.

0636   Coanda, Richard.   Hopkins and Donne: "Mystic" and Metaphysical.   Renascence, 9: 180—187.

0637   Cobb, Lucille S.   John Donne and the Common Law. DA, 17: 1082.

0638   Cunningham, J. S.   At Donne's Death Bed.   Durham University Journal, 18: 28.

0639   Emerson, Katherine T.   Two Problems in Donne's "Farewell to Love."   MLN, 72: 93—95.

0640   Empson, William.   Donne the Space Man.   KR, 19: 337—399.

0641   Gardner, Helen.   Another Note on Donne: "Since she whome I lov'd."   MLR, 52: 564—565.

0642   Hagopian, John V.   Some Cruxes in Donne's Poetry. N&Q, N.S. 4: 500—502.

0643   Hall, Vernon, Jr.   Donne's "Satyre" II, 71—72.   Explicator, 15: 24.

0644   Hilberry, Conrad.   The First Stanza of Donne's "Hymne to God my God, in my Sicknesse."   N&Q, N.S. 4: 336—337.

0645   Kermode, Frank.   John Donne. (The British Council).   London, Longmans, Green.   48 p.

0646   Legouis, Pierre.   Donne, l'Amour et les Critiques. Études Anglaises, 10: 115—122.

0647   Mabbott, Thomas O.   Donne's "Satyre II," 71—72. Explicator, 16: 19.

0648   Madison, Arthur L.   Explication of John Donne's "The Flea."   N&Q, N.S. 4: 60—61.

0649   Main, C. F.   New Texts of John Donne.   SB, 9: 225—233.

0650   Malloch, A. E.   The Definition of Sin in Donne's Biathanatos.   MLN, 72: 332—335.

0651   Mazzeo, Joseph A.   Notes on John Donne's Alchemical Imagery.   Isis, 48: 103—123.

JOHN DONNE

Nathanson, Leonard. The Context of Dryden's 0652
Criticism of Donne's and Cowley's Love Poetry.
N&Q, N.S. 4: 56—59.

Nathanson, Leonard. Dryden, Donne, and Cowley. 0653
N&Q, N.S. 4: 197—198.

Novarr, David. The Dating of Donne's La Corona. 0654
PQ, 36: 259—265.

P., R. Jonson's "To John Donne." Explicator, 16: 0655
Q5.

Parish, John E. Donne as a Petrarchan. N&Q, 0656
N.S. 4: 377—378.

Smith, A. J. Donne in His Time: A Reading of 0657
"The Extasie." Rivista di Letterature Moderne
e Comparate (Firenze), 10: 260—275.

Smith, A. J. Sources of Difficulty and of Value 0658
in the Poetry of John Donne. Letterature Moderne, 7: 182—190.

Warnke, Frank J. Donne's "The Anniversarie." 0659
Explicator, 16: 12.

Whitlock, Baird W. [Correction of transcript of 0660
Edward Alleyn's letter to John Donne.] RES,
N.S. 8: 420—421. See: RES, N.S. 6: 365—371.

1958

Combellack, Frederick M. Jonson's "To John 0661
Donne." Explicator, 17: 6.

Cross, K. Gustav. Another Donne Allusion. N&Q, 0662
N.S. 5: 532—533.

Donne, John. The Poems of John Donne. Intro- 0663
duction by Hugh I'Anson Fausset. (Everyman
Library). London, Dent. 290 p.

Donne, John. Selected Poems of John Donne. 0664
Edited by James Reeves. New York, Macmillan.
xviii, 108 p.

Donne, John. The Sermons of John Donne. Se- 0665
lected and Introduction by Theodore A. Gill.
New York, Meridian Books. 288 p.

Falk, Ruth E. Donne's "Resurrection, Imperfect." 0666
Explicator, 17: 24.

Hagopian, John V. A Difficult Crux in Donne's 0667
Satyre II. MLN, 73: 255—257.

Hagopian, John V. Donne's "Love's Diet," 20— 0668

24. Explicator, 17: 5.

0669 Hickey, Robert L. Donne's Art of Memory. Tennessee Studies in Literature, 3: 29—36.

0670 Howarth, R. G. References to John Donne. N&Q, N.S. 5: 43.

0671 Joseph, Brother, FSC. Donne's "A Valediction: Forbidding Mourning," 1—8. Explicator, 16: 43.

0672 Kawasaki, Toshihiko. John Donne's Religious Poetry and the New Criticism. DA, 18: 1047.

0673 Keynes, Geoffrey. A Bibliography of Dr. John Donne. 3rd edn. Cambridge, Cambridge University. xviii, 285 p.

0674 Keynes, Geoffrey. Dr. Donne and Scaliger. TLS, February 21, pp. 93, 108.

0675 Legouis, Pierre. John Donne and William Cowper. Anglia, 76: 536—538.

0676 Lowe, Irving. Both Centers One: The Reason-Faith Equation in Donne's Sermons. DA, 18: 590—591.

0677 Macklem, Michael. The Anatomy of the World: Relations Between Natural and Moral Law from Donne to Pope. Minneapolis, University of Minnesota. 139 p.

0678 Marshall, William H. Elizabeth Drury and the Heathens. N&Q, N.S. 5: 533—534.

0679 Marshall, William H. A Possible Interpretation of Donne's "The Second Anniversary," (Lines 33—36). N&Q, N.S. 5: 540—541.

0680 Masood-al-Hasan. Donne's Imagery. Aligarh, Muslim University. 95 p.

0681 Murray, W. A. Donne's Gold-Leaf and His Compasses. MLN, 73: 329—330.

0682 Patrides, C. A. Milton and His Contemporaries on the Chains of Satan. MLN, 73: 257—260.

0683 Powers, Doris C. Donne's Compass. RES, N.S. 9: 173—175.

0684 Praz, Mario. John Donne. Torino, S.A.I.E. 277 p.

0685 Quinn, Dennis B. John Donne's Sermons and the Psalms and the Traditions of Biblical Exegesis. DA, 18: 2131—2132.

0686 Richmond, H. M. Donne and Ronsard. N&Q, N.S. 5: 534—536.

JOHN DONNE

pp. 279—306. Oxford, Clarendon.

0706 Manley, Francis. Chaucer's Rosary and Donne's Bracelet: Ambiguous Coral. MLN, 74: 385—388.

0707 Martz, Louis L. Donne and the Meditative Tradition. Thought, 34: 269—278.

0708 Moran, Berna. Donne's Poem "The Dream." Litera, 6: 31—33.

0709 Murray, W. A. What was the Soul of the Apple? RES, N.S. 10: 141—155.

0710 Newton, Willoughby. A Study of John Donne's Sonnet XIV. Anglican Theological Review, 41: 10—12.

0711 Pafford, J. H. P. Donne: An Early Nineteenth-Century Estimate. N&Q, N.S. 6: 131—132.

0712 Peterson, Douglas L. John Donne's Holy Sonnets and the Anglican Doctrine of Contrition. SP, 56: 504—518.

0713 Praz, Mario. Donne and Dickens. TLS, February 20, p. 97.

0714 Richmond, H. M. The Intangible Mistress. MP, 56: 217—223.

0715 Scott, Robert I. Donne and Kepler. N&Q, N.S. 6: 208—209.

0716 Stephenson, A. A. Gerard Manley Hopkins and John Donne. Downside Review, 77: 300—320.

0717 Tillotson, Kathleen. Donne's Poetry in the Nineteenth Century (1800—1872). In Elizabethan and Jacobean Studies, pp. 307—326. Oxford, Clarendon.

0718 White, William. Sir Geoffrey Keynes's Bibliography of John Donne: A Review with Addenda. Bulletin of Bibliography, 22: 186—189.

0719 Whitlock, Baird D. The Heredity and Childhood of John Donne. N&Q, N.S. 6: 257—262, 348—353.

1960

0720 Allen, Don Cameron. The Genesis of Donne's Dreams. MLN, 75: 293—295.

0721 Anon. Liebeslied. Frankfurter Hefte, 1: 90.

0722 Bauerle, R. F. John Donne Redone and Undone. N&Q, N.S. 7: 386.

0723 Campo, Cristina. Tre Versioni da John Donne.

JOHN DONNE

Paragone, 11 (no. 128): 71—73.

Candelaria, Frederick H.   Ovid and the Indifferent   0724
Lovers. RN, 13: 294—297.

Chambers, A. B.   The Meaning of the "Temple" in   0725
Donne's La Corona. JEGP, 59: 212—217.

Combecher, Hans.   John Donne's "Annunciation":   0726
Eine Interpretation. Die Neueren Sprachen,
N.S. 9: 488—492.

Crossett, John.   Bacon and Donne. N&Q, N.S. 7:   0727
386—387.

Duncan-Jones, E. E.   The Barren Plane-Tree in   0728
Donne's "The Autumnall." N&Q, N.S. 7: 53.

Durr, Robert A.   Donne's "The Primrose." JEGP,   0729
59: 218—222.

Ellrodt, Robert.   Chronologie des poèmes de Donne.   0730
Études Anglaises, 13: 452—463.

Esch, Arno.   Paradise and Calvary. Anglia, 78:   0731
74—77.

Fox, Robert C.   Donne in the British West Indies.   0732
History of Ideas News Letter, 5: 77—80.

Gardner, Helen.   Donne MSS for the Bodleian.   0733
TLS, March 11, p. 168.

Grenander, M. E.   "Holy Sonnets" VIII and XVII: 0734
John Donne. Boston University Studies in English, 4: 95—105.

Holloway, John.   The Charted Mirror. London,   0735
Routledge. 226 p.

Hughes, Merritt Y.   Some of Donne's "Ecstasies."   0736
PMLA, 75: 509—518.

Kawasaki, Toshihiko.   John Donne's Microcosm: 0737
Some Queries to Professor Empson. Studies in
English Literature (Tokyo) 36: 229—250.

Kuhnre, W. W.   Exposition of Sin in the Sermons   0738
of John Donne. Lutheran Quarterly, 12: 217—
234.

Martz, Louis L.   John Donne: The Meditative   0739
Voice. Massachusetts Review, 1: 326—342.

Morgan, Bayard Q.   Compulsory Patterns in Poetry.   0740
PMLA, 75: 634—635.

Poynter, F. N. L.   John Donne and William Harvey.   0741
Journal of the History of Medicine and Allied
Sciences, 15: 233—246.

0742   Quinn, Dennis B.   Donne and "Tyr."   MLN, 75:
       643—644.
0743   Quinn, Dennis B.   Donne's Christian Eloquence.
       ELH, 27: 276—297.
0744   Sloan, Thomas O., Jr.   The Rhetoric in the Poetry
       of John Donne.   DA, 21: 1557.
0745   Smith, A. J.   New Bearings in Donne: Aire and An-
       gels.   English, 13: 49—53.
0746   Sowton, Ian.   Religious Opinion in the Prose Let-
       ters of John Donne.   Canadian Journal of The-
       ology, 6: 179—190.
0747   Stein, Arnold.   Donne and the 1920's: A Problem in
       Historical Consciousness.   ELH, 27: 16—29.
0748   Vordtriede, Werner.   "La Corona."   Die Neue Rund-
       schau, 71: 485—488.
0749   Webber, Joan Mary.   Contrary Music: A Study of
       the Prose Styles of John Donne.   DA, 20: 4117.
0750   Whitlock, Baird W.   The Family of John Donne,
       1588—1591.   N&Q, N.S. 7: 380—386.
0751   Williamson, George.   Seventeenth Century Con-
       texts.   London, Faber and Faber.   291 p.
0752   Zimmerman, Donald E.   The Nature of Man: John
       Donne's Songs and Holy Sonnets. (Emporia State
       Research Studies, v. 8, no. 3). Emporia, Kansas
       State Teachers College.   33 p.

EDWARD, LORD HERBERT
OF CHERBURY

1941

Aaron, R. I.   The "Autobiography" of Edward, First   0753
Lord Herbert of Cherbury: The Original Manuscript Material. MLR, 36: 184—194.

Dunlap, Rhodes.   Thomas Carew, Thomas Carey,   0754
and "The Sovereign of the Seas." MLN, 56:
268—271.

Willey, Basil.   Lord Herbert of Cherbury: A Spir-   0755
itual Quixote of the Seventeenth Century. Essays and Studies, 27: 22—29.

1942

Hanford, James H.   Lord Herbert of Cherbury and   0756
His Son. HLQ, 5: 317—332.

1944

Herbert, Edward.   Lord Herbert of Cherbury's De   0757
Religione Laici.   Edited and translated by Harold
R. Hutcheson. New Haven, Yale University.
x, 199 p.

1946

Keister, Don A.   Lady Kent and the Two Sir Ed-   0758
wards. MLN, 61: 169—172.

1947

Keister, Don A.   The Birth Date of Lord Herbert of   0759
Cherbury. MLN, 62: 389—393.

Keister, Don A.   Donne and Herbert of Cherbury: 0760
An Exchange of Verses. MLQ, 8: 430—434.

EDWARD, LORD HERBERT

0761   Rossi, Mario Manlio.   La Vita, le Opere, i Tempi di
        Edoardo Herbert di Chirbùry. 3 vols. Firenze,
        G. C. Sansoni.

1948

0762   Lanchester, H. C.   The Birth Date of Lord Herbert
        of Cherbury. MLN, 63: 144.

1953

0763   Harrison, John L.   Lord Herbert's Two Sonnets on
        Black. N&Q, 198: 323—325.

1954

0764   Warnke, Frank J.   This Metaphysick Lord: A Study
        of the Poetry of Herbert of Cherbury. DA, 14: 1738.
0765   Warnke, Frank J.   Two Previously Unnoted MSS. of
        Poems by Lord Herbert of Cherbury. N&Q, N.S.
        1: 141—142.

1956

0766   Sprott, S. Ernest.   The Osler Manuscript of Her-
        bert's Religio Laici. The Library, 5th ser. 11:
        120—122.

1957

0767   Dart, Thurston.   Lord Herbert of Cherbury's Lute-
        Book. Music and Letters, 38: 136—148.
0768   Merchant, W. Moelwyn.   Lord Herbert of Cherbury
        and Seventeenth-Century Historical Writing.
        Transactions of the Honourable Society of Cymm-
        rodorion, pp. 47—63.
0769   Rossi, Mario Manlio.   Herbert of Cherbury's Re-
        ligio Laici: A Bibliographical Note. Edinburgh
        Bibliographical Society Transactions, 4 (pt. 2;
        1956—1957, pub. 1962): 45—52.

1958

0770   Bottrall, Margaret.   Every Man a Phoenix. Studies
        in Seventeenth-Century Autobiography. London,
        John Murray. 174 p.
0771   Rickey, Mary Ellen.   Rhymecraft in Edward and
        George Herbert. JEGP, 57: 502—511.

GEORGE HERBERT

1939

Brown, R. Goulding.   A Herbert Query. TLS, July 8,   0772
p. 406.

Coulter, C. C.   A Possible Classical Source for   0773
the Blackamoor Maid. PQ, 18: 409—410.

Hutchinson, F. E.   The First Edition of Herbert's   0774
Temple. Papers of the Oxford Bibliographical
Society, 5: 187—197.

Hutchinson, F. E.   Missing Herbert Manuscripts.   0775
TLS, July 15, p. 421.

Murry, J. Middleton.   A Herbert Query. TLS, July   0776
1, p. 390.

Rattray, R. F.   A Herbert Query. TLS, June 24, p.   0777
374.

Taketomo, Sofu.   Metaphysical Poetry of George   0778
Herbert. Studies in English Literature (Tokyo),
19: 155—172.

Thompson, Elbert N. S.   The Temple and The Chris-   0779
tian Year. PMLA, 54: 1018—1025.

1940

Reese, Harold.   A Borrower from Quarles and Her-   0780
bert. MLN, 55: 50—52.

1941

Anon.   George Herbert. N&Q, 180: 288.   0781

Curr, H. S.   George Herbert. TLS, August 2, pp.   0782
371, 397.

F., R.   George Herbert's "A Parodie." N&Q, 180:   0783
334.

GEORGE HERBERT

0784   Freeman, Rosemary.   George Herbert and the Emblem
        Books. RES, 17: 150—165.
0785   Freeman, Rosemary.   George Herbert's Songs. TLS,
        July 12, pp. 334, 337.
0786   H., C. E.   A Query from Herbert. N&Q, 181: 246.
0787   Herbert, George.   The Works of George Herbert.
        Edited by F. E. Hutchinson. Oxford, Clarendon.
        lxxvii, 619 p.
0788   Selincourt, Ernest de.   George Herbert. Hibbert
        Journal, 39: 389—397.
0789   Shewring, W.   George Herbert. Dublin Review, 209:
        213—214.

1942

0790   Bradbrook, M. C.   The Liturgical Tradition in Eng-
        lish Verse: George Herbert and T. S. Eliot. The-
        ology, 45: 13—23.
0791   Grierson, H. J. C.   Hutchinson's Edition of George
        Herbert. MLR, 37: 207—214.
0792   Rowse, A. L.   The Caroline Country Parson: George
        Herbert's Ideal. Country Life, February 6, pp.
        252—255.

1943

0793   L., E. W.   Herbert's "The Collar." Explicator, 2:
        Q16.
0794   McLuhan, Herbert M.   Herbert's "Vertue." Expli-
        cator, 2: 4.
0795   Miles, Josephine.   Some Major Poetic Words. Es-
        says and Studies (Berkeley), 14: 233—239.
0796   Wilson, F. P.   A Note on George Herbert's "The
        Quidditie." RES, 19: 398—399.

1944

0797   Agatha, M.   George Herbert: Poet of Right Inten-
        tion. Ave Maria, 59: 327—330.
0798   Allen, Don Cameron.   George Herbert's Sycomore.
        MLN, 59: 493—495.
0799   D., G. H.   George Herbert and Dante. N&Q, 187:
        81.
0800   Douds, J. B.   George Herbert's Use of the Trans-
        ferred Verb: A Study in the Structure of Poetic

GEORGE HERBERT

Imagery. MLQ, 5: 163—174.
Eliot, T. S.   What is Minor Poetry?   Welsh Review,   0801
  3: 256—267.
Howarth, R. G.   George Herbert.   N&Q, 187: 122.   0802
Knights, L. C.   George Herbert.   Scrutiny, 12:   0803
  171—186.
Mabbott, Thomas O.   Herbert's "The Collar."   Ex-   0804
  plicator, 3: 12.
Norton, Dan S.   Herbert's "The Collar."   Explica-   0805
  tor, 2: 41.

1945

Mead, D. S.   Herbert's "The Pulley."   Explicator,   0806
  4: 17.
Norton, Dan S.   Herbert's "The Collar."   Expli-   0807
  cator, 3: 46.
Oliver, Peter.   George Herbert (1595—1633).   0808
  Action, December, pp. 9—12.

1946

Tannenbaum, Samuel A. and Dorothy R. Tannenbaum.   0809
  George Herbert: A Concise Bibliography. New
  York, S. A. Tannenbaum.   52 p.
Wilson, F. P.   English Proverbs and Dictionaries   0810
  of Proverbs. The Library, 4th ser., 26: 51—71.

1947

Ferguson, F. S.   "The Temple."   TLS, May 3, p.   0811
  211.
Ross, Malcolm M.   George Herbert and the Hu-   0812
  manist Tradition.   UTQ, 16: 169—182.

1948

Warren, Austin.   Rage for Order: Essays in Criti-   0813
  cism.   Chicago, University of Chicago.   ix,
  164 p.

1949

Cropper, M.   Flame Touches Flame.   London, Long-   0814
  mans, Green.   xv, 225 p.
Gibbs, J.   An Unknown Poem of George Herbert.   0815
  TLS, December 30, p. 857.

GEORGE HERBERT

0816   Herbert, George.   George Herbert's Country Parson.
        Edited by G. M. Forbes. London, Faith. xiv, 56 p.

1950

0817   Benjamin, Edwin B.   Herbert's "Vertue." Explicator,
        9: 12.
0818   Empson, William.   George Herbert and Miss Tuve.
        KR, 12: 735—738.
0819   Tuve, Rosemond.   On Herbert's "Sacrifice." KR,
        12: 51—75.
0820   Zitner, Sheldon P.   Herbert's "Jordan" Poems. Ex-
        plicator, 9: 11.

1951

0821   Bickham, Jack M.   Herbert's "The Collar." Expli-
        cator, 10: 17.
0822   Blackburn, William.   Lady Magdalen Herbert and
        Her Son George.   South Atlantic Quarterly, 50:
        378—388.
0823   Herbert, George.   Four Poems of Herbert. Trans-
        lated by Joseph H. Summers. Quarterly Review
        of Literature, 6: 211—212.
0824   Silver, Louis H.   The First Edition of Walton's Life
        of Herbert. Harvard Library Bulletin, 5: 371—372.
0825   Summers, Joseph H.   Herbert's Form. PMLA, 66:
        1055—1072.

1952

0826   Baruch, F. R.   Donne and Herbert. TLS, May 30,
        p. 361.
0827   Bottrall, Margaret.   George Herbert and "The
        Country Parson." Listener, 47: 558—559.
0828   D., A.   Five Notes on George Herbert. N&Q, 197:
        420—422.
0829   Eldredge, Frances.   Herbert's "Jordan." Explicator,
        11: 3.
0830   Leishman, J. B.   Donne and Herbert. TLS, June 13,
        p. 391.
0831   Summers, Joseph H.   Herbert's "Trinitie Sunday."
        Explicator, 10: 23.
0832   Tuve, Rosemond.   A Reading of George Herbert.
        Chicago, University of Chicago. 215 p.

GEORGE HERBERT

1953

Burke, Kenneth. On Covery, Re- & Dis-Accent, 13: 0833
218—226.
Knieger, Bernard. Herbert's "Redemption." Expli- 0834
cator, 11: 24.
Leach, Elsie A. John Wesley's Use of George 0835
Herbert. HLQ, 16: 183—202.
Noakes, Aubrey. The Mother of George Herbert. 0836
Contemporary Review, 183: 39—45.
Thornton, Robert D. Polyphiloprogenitive: The 0837
Sapient Stulers. Anglican Theological Review,
35: 28—36.

1954

Akrigg, G. P. V. George Herbert's "Caller." N&Q, 0838
N.S. 1: 17.
Bottrall, Margaret. George Herbert. London, John 0839
Murray. 153 p.
Emslie, Macdonald. Herbert's "Jordan" I. Expli- 0840
cator, 12: 35.
Moloney, Michael F. A Suggested Gloss for Her- 0841
bert's "Box Where Sweets . . ." N&Q, N.S. 1:
50.
Ross, Malcolm M. Poetry and Dogma. New Bruns- 0842
wick, Rutgers University. xii, 256 p.
Summers, Joseph H. George Herbert: His Reli- 0843
gion and His Art. Cambridge, Harvard Univer-
sity. 246 p.
Whan, Edgar William. George Herbert's The 0844
Temple: A Critical Essay Toward a Synoptic
Reading. DA, 14: 668.
Young, Simon. George Herbert. TLS, January 15, 0845
p. 41.

1955

Davenport, A. George Herbert and Ovid. N&Q, 0846
N.S. 2: 98.
Duncan-Jones, E. E. Benlowes's Borrowings from 0847
George Herbert. RES, N.S. 6: 179—180.
Levang, Lewis Dwight. Structure in a Winding 0848
Stair: A Study of George Herbert. DA, 15: 2191—
2192.

0849   Wickes, George. George Herbert's Views on Poetry.
Revue des Langues Vivantes (Bruxelles), 21: 344—
352.

1956

0850   Herbert, George. The Country Parson and Selected
Poems. (Treasury of Christian Books Series).
London, S.C.M. Press. 125 p.
0851   Hilberry, Conrad. Two Cruxes in George Herbert's
"Redemption." N&Q, N.S. 3: 514.
0852   Koretz, Gene H. The Rhyme Scheme in Herbert's
"Man." N&Q, N.S. 3: 144—146.
0853   Manning, Stephen. Herbert's "The Pearl," 38. Explicator, 14: 25.

1957

0854   Boyd, George Wilson. George Herbert: A Revalua-
tion. DA, 17: 1747.
0855   Collmer, Robert G. Herbert's "Businesse," 15—30.
Explicator, 16: 11.
0856   Levang, Lewis Dwight. George Herbert's "The
Church Militant" and the Chances of History.
PQ, 36: 265—268.
0857   Moloney, Michael F. A Note on Herbert's "Season'd
Timber." N&Q, N.S. 4: 434—435.
0858   Taylor, Ivan E. Cavalier Sophistication in the Poetry of George Herbert. Anglican Theological
Review, 39: 229—243.

1958

0859   Adler, Jacob H. Form and Meaning in Herbert's
"Discipline." N&Q, N.S. 5: 240—243.
0860   Evans, G. Blakemore. George Herbert's "Jordan."
N&Q, N.S. 5: 215.
0861   Hilberry, Conrad. Herbert's "Dooms-day." Explicator, 16: 24.
0862   Joselyn, Sister M. Herbert and Hopkins: Two
Lyrics. Renascence, 10: 192—195.
0863   Rickey, Mary Ellen. Rhymecraft in Edward and
George Herbert. JEGP, 57: 502—511.

GEORGE HERBERT

1959

Chute, Marchette. Two Gentle Men: The Lives   0864
of George Herbert and Robert Herrick. New
York, Dutton. 319 p.

Kimmey, John L.   The Art of the Particular—A Con-   0865
sideration of George Herbert's Revisions. SCN,
17: 28—29.

1960

Herbert, George. Poems of George Herbert. In-   0866
troduction by Helen Gardner. (World Classics).
Oxford, Oxford University. xxi, 285 p.

Herbert, George.   Selected Poems of George Her-   0867
bert. Edited by Douglas Brown. London, Hutchinson. 159 p.

Knieger, Bernard.   The Religious Verse of George   0868
Herbert. College Language Association Journal, 4: 138—147.

Leach, Elsie A.   Lydgate's "The Dolerous Pyte   0869
of Crystes Passioun" and Herbert's "The Sacrifice." N&Q, N.S. 7: 421.

Leach, Elsie A.   More Seventeenth-Century Ad-   0870
mirers of Herbert. N&Q, N.S. 7: 62—63.

Montgomery, Robert L., Jr.   The Province of Alle-   0871
gory in George Herbert's Verse. Texas Studies
in Literature and Language, 1: 457—472.

Stambler, Elizabeth.   The Unity of Herbert's   0872
"Temple." Cross Currents, 10: 251—266.

Tuve, Rosemond.   George Herbert and "Caritas."   0873
Journal of the Warburg and Courtauld Institute,
22: 303—331.

HENRY KING

1945

Hammond, Geraldine.   The Poetry of Bishop Henry   0874
King.   University of Colorado Studies, 27: 47—
48.

1952

Simpson, Percy.   John and Henry King: A Correc-   0875
tion.   Bodleian Library Record, 4: 208—209.

1954

Gleckner, Robert F.   King's "The Exequy." Expli-   0876
cator, 12: 46.

1956

Gleckner, Robert F.   Henry King: A Poet of his   0877
Age.   Wisconsin Academy of Sciences, Arts and
Letters, 45: 149—167.

1960

King, Henry.   Poems.   Edited by James Rupert Baker.   0878
Denver, A. Swallow.   138 p.

ANDREW MARVELL

1939

Bradbrook, M. C. and M. G. Lloyd Thomas. Mar-   0879
vell and the Concept of Metamorphosis. The
Criterion, 18: 236—254.

Putt, S. Gorley. Mosaiques of the Air: A Note on   0880
Andrew Marvell. English, 2: 366—375.

1940

Brooks, Harold F. Authorship of "Britannia and   0881
Rawleigh": Additional Evidence Against Ascrip-
tion to Marvell. N&Q, 179: 146.

Bradbrook, M. C. and M. G. Lloyd Thomas. An-   0882
drew Marvell. Cambridge, Cambridge University. viii, 161 p.

De Beer, E. S. Dryden: "The Kind Keeper." The   0883
"Poet of Scandalous Memory." N&Q, 179: 128—
129.

1941

Bradbrook, M. C. Marvell and the Poetry of Rural   0884
Solitude. RES, 17: 37—46.

Warner, Oliver. Mars and Euterpe: An Echo   0885
Across Three Centuries. Blackwoods Magazine, 250: 512—517.

1942

Marvell, Andrew. Poems. Mt. Vernon, New York,   0886
Peter Pauper. 117 p.

Roberts, John H. Marvell's "To His Coy Mis-   0887
tress." Explicator, 1: 17.

ANDREW MARVELL

1943

0888 Daniel, Robert. Marvell's "To His Coy Mistress."
Explicator, 1: 37.

1945

0889 Anon. A Note on the Purchase of MS Eng. Poet.
d. 49. Bodleian Library Record, 2: 125.
0890 Rainbow, M. F. E. Marvell and Nature. Durham
University Journal, 6: 22—27.
0891 Sedgwick, A. Andrew Marvell. TLS, October 27,
p. 511.

1946

0892 Bradbrook, M. C. and M. G. Lloyd Thomas. Andrew
Marvell. TLS, January 5, p. 7.
0893 Davies, Godfrey. The Date of "Brittania and Rawleigh." HLQ, 9: 311—318.
0894 Orwen, William R. Andrew Marvell's "The Garden." N&Q, 191: 247—249.
0895 Reynolds, Lorna. Andrew Marvell. Dublin Magazine, 21: 10—18.

1947

0896 Bland, D. S. Marvell and Massinger: A Source of
"The Definition of Love." RES, 23: 267.
0897 Brooks, Cleanth. Criticism and Literary History:
Marvell's "Horatian Ode." In English Institute
Essays, pp. 129—158. New York, Columbia University. Also published in: SR, 55: 199—222.
0898 Legouis, Pierre. Marvell and Massinger: A Source
of "The Definition of Love." RES, 23: 63—65.

1948

0899 Fussell, E. S. Milton's "Two-handed Engine" Yet
Once More. N&Q, 193: 338—339.
0900 Walton, Geoffrey. The Poetry of Marvell: A Sum-
ming Up. Politics and Letters, 1 (no. 4): 22—35.

1949

0901 De Beer, E. S. "Nostradamus's Prophecy." N&Q,
194: 360—362.

ANDREW MARVELL

Duncan-Jones, E. E.   Marvell in 1656.   TLS, De-   0902
cember 2, p. 791.
Marvell, Andrew.   Selected Poems.   Edited by Fred   0903
Marnau.   (Crown Classics).   London, Grey Walls.
64 p.
Turner, W. Arthur.   Milton, Marvell and "Dradon"   0904
at Cromwell's Funeral.   PQ, 28: 320—323.

1950

Duncan-Jones, E. E.   Marvell in 1656.   TLS, Jan-   0905
uary 13, p. 25.
Garvin, Katharine.   Andrew Marvell the Anchorite.   0906
TLS, August 11, p. 508.
Klonsky, Milton.   A Guide Through "The Garden."   0907
SR, 58: 16—35.
Margoliouth, H. M.   Marvell's "Thyrsis and Do-   0908
rinda."   TLS, May 19, p. 309.

1951

Henn, T. R.   The Apple and the Spectroscope.   0909
London, Methuen.   165 p.
Hyman, Lawrence W.   The Lyric Poetry of Andrew   0910
Marvell.   Microfilm Abstracts, 11: 683—684.
McChesney, John.   Marvell's "The Garden."   Ex-   0911
plicator, 10: 4.
Macdonald, Hugh.   Andrew Marvell's Miscellan-   0912
eous Poems, 1681.   TLS, July 13, p. 444.
Macdonald, Hugh.   Marvell's Miscellaneous   0913
Poems, 1681.   TLS, August 24, p. 533.
Martin, L. C.   Marvell, Massinger and Sidney.   0914
RES, N.S. 2: 374—375.
Muir, Kenneth.   A Virgilian Echo in Marvell.   N&Q,   0915
196: 115.
Orwen, William R.   Marvell and Buckingham.   0916
N&Q, 196: 10—11.
Proudfoot, L.   Marvell: Sallust and the Horatian   0917
Ode.   N&Q, 196: 434.

1952

Ames, R.   Decadence in the Art of T. S. Eliot.   0918
Science and Society, 16: 193—221.
Blakiston, Noel.   Andrew Marvell at Eton.   TLS,   0919

February 8, p. 109.

0920 Bühler, C. F.   A Letter by Andrew Marvell. N&Q,
197: 451.

0921 Bush, Douglas.   Marvell's "Horatian Ode." SR,
60: 363—376.

0922 Carswell, John.   A Civilized Poet.   TLS, August 1,
p. 501.

0923 Cutts, John P.   Marvell's "Thyrsis and Dorinda."
TLS, August 8, p. 517.

0924 Devlin, Christopher.   Ariel. The Tablet, June 28,
p. 520.

0925 Keister, Don A.   Marvell's "The Garden." Explicator, 10: 24.

0926 Kermode, Frank.   The Argument of Marvell's "Garden." EIC, 2: 225—241.

0927 Kermode, Frank.   Two Notes on Marvell. N&Q,
197: 136—138, 218.

0928 Lawson, John.   Andrew Marvell. TLS, September
26, p. 629.

0929 Le Comte, Edward S.   Marvell's "The Nymph Complaining for the Death of Her Fawn." MP, 50:
97—101.

0930 Macdonald, Hugh.   Andrew Marvell. TLS, October
10, p. 661.

0931 Marvell, Andrew.   The Poems of Andrew Marvell.
Edited by Hugh Macdonald. (Muses Library).
London, Routledge. xxx, 206 p. 2nd edn. issued
in 1956.

0932 Marvell, Andrew.   The Poems and Letters of Andrew Marvell. Edited by H. M. Margoliouth.
2nd edn. 2 vols. Oxford, Clarendon.

0933 Marvell, Andrew.   Selected Poetry and Prose of
Andrew Marvell. Edited by Dennis Davison.
London, Harrap. 246 p.

0934 Simeone, William.   A Probable Antecedent of Marvell's "Horatian Ode." N&Q, 197: 316—318.

1953

0935 Brooks, Cleanth.   A Note on the Limits of "History"
and the Limits of "Criticism." SR, 61: 129—135.

0936 Day, Robert A.   Marvell's "Glew." PQ, 32: 344—
346.

Duncan-Jones, E. E.   Milton and Marvell. TLS,   0937
July 31, p. 493.
Duncan-Jones, E. E.   Notes on Marvell. N&Q,   0938
198: 102, 430—431.
Duncan-Jones, E. E.   T. C. of "A Prospect of Flow-   0939
ers." TLS, October 30, p. 693.
Gwynn, Frederick L.   Marvell's "To His Coy Mis-   0940
tress," 33—46. Explicator, 11: 49.
Howarth, R. G.   Marvell: An Emendation. N&Q,   0941
198: 330.
Legouis, Pierre.   La Purge de Gargantua ou Mar-   0942
vell et Tallemant des Réaux. Études Anglaises,
6: 236—238.
Margoliouth, H. M.   Notes on Marvell. N&Q, 198:   0943
220.
Sleigh, Gordon F.   Bibliographical Notes: The   0944
Authorship of William and Margaret. The Li-
brary, 5th ser., 8: 121—123.
Smith, Harold W.   Cowley, Marvell and the Sec-   0945
ond Temple. Scrutiny, 19: 184—205.
Summers, Joseph H.   Marvell's "Nature." ELH,   0946
20: 121—135.
Winny, James.   A Marvell Emendation. TLS, Octo-   0947
ber 2, p. 629.
Withington, Eleanor.   Marvell and Montague: 0948
Another Source for "The Definition of Love."
RES, N.S. 4: 261—263.

1954

Lucht, William Edward.   Andrew Marvell: An In-   0949
terpretation. DA, 14: 2336—2337.
Williamson, Karina.   Marvell's "The Nymph Com-   0950
plaining for the Death of Her Fawn": A Reply.
MP, 51: 268—271.

1955

Davison, Dennis.   A Marvell Allusion in Ward's   0951
Diary. N&Q, N.S. 2: 22.
Davison, Dennis.   Marvell and Politics. N&Q,   0952
N.S. 2: 201—202.
Davison, Dennis.   Marvell's "The Definition of   0953
Love." RES, N.S. 6: 141—146.

0954 Duncan-Jones, E. E.   Marvell and the Cinque
Ports. TLS, November 11, p. 673.
0955 Ehrenpreis, I.   Four of Swift's Sources.   MLN, 70:
95—100.
0956 Emerson, Everett H.   Andrew Marvell's The Nymph
Complaining for the Death of Her Faun.   Études
Anglaises, 8: 107—110.
0957 Foster, Ruel E.   A Tonal Study: Marvell.   University of Kansas City Review, 22: 73—78.
0958 Lerner, L. D.   Andrew Marvell: "An Horatian Ode
Upon Cromwell's Return from Ireland."   In In-
terpretations, pp. 59—74.   London, Routledge
and Kegan Paul.
0959 Orwen, William R.   Marvell's "Bergamot."   N&Q,
N.S. 2: 340—341.
0960 O[r]wen, William R.   Marvell's "Narrow Case."
N&Q, N.S. 2: 201.
0961 Røstvig, Maren-Sofie.   Benlowes, Marvell and the
Divine Casimire.   HLQ, 18: 13—35.
0962 Schmitter, Dean Morgan.   Andrew Marvell: Member
from Hull; A Study in the Ecclesiastical and
Political Thought of the Restoration.   DA, 15:
1064—1065.
0963 Senn, G. T.   The Text of Marvell's Poems.   N&Q,
N.S. 2: 302.

1956

0964 Allen, Don Cameron.   Marvell's "Nymph."   ELH,
23: 93—111.
0965 Duncan-Jones, E. E.   Marvell His Own Critic.
N&Q, N.S. 3: 383—384.
0966 Farnham, Anthony E.   Saint Teresa and the Coy Mistress.   Boston University Studies in English, 2:
226—239.
0967 Hyman, Lawrence W.   "Ideas" in Marvell's Lyric
Poetry.   History of Ideas News Letter, 2: 29—
31.
0968 Kermode, Frank.   Definitions of Love.   RES, N.S.
7: 183—185.
0969 Orwen, William R.   A Study of Marvell's "Horatian
Ode."   DA, 16: 1907.
0970 Sasek, Lawrence A.   Marvell's "To His Coy Mis-

tress," 45—46. Explicator, 14: 47.

Sedelow, Walter A., Jr.   Marvell's <u>To His Coy Mis-</u>   0971
<u>tress.</u> MLN, 71: 6—8.

Wheatcroft, John.   Andrew Marvell and the Winged   0972
Chariot.   Bucknell Review, 6 (no. 3): 22—53.

1957

Carens, James F.   Andrew Marvell's Cromwell   0973
Poems.   Bucknell Review, 7: 41—70.

Colie, Rosalie L.   Marvell's "Bermudas" and the   0974
Puritan Paradise.   RN, 10: 75—79.

Duncan-Jones, E. E.   Benlowes, Marvell and The   0975
Divine Casimire: A Note.   HLQ, 20: 183—184.

Duncan-Jones, E. E.   Marvell's "Friend in Persia."   0976
N&Q, N.S. 4: 466—467.

Duncan-Jones, E. E.   Marvell's "Inscribenda Lu-   0977
parae."   TLS, April 26, p. 257.

Grundy, Joan.   Marvell's Grasshoppers.   N&Q,   0978
N.S. 4: 142.

Iser, Wolfgang.   Andrew Marvell "To His Coy   0979
Mistress."   Die Neuren Sprachen, N.S. 6: 555—
577.

Isham, Gyles.   Abram van den Bampde.   N&Q,   0980
N.S. 4: 461—463.

Legouis, Pierre.   Marvell and the New Critics.   0981
RES, N.S. 8: 382—389.

Legouis, Pierre.   Marvell's "Inscribenda Luparae."   0982
TLS, October 4, p. 593.

Robbins, Caroline.   Carlisle and Marvell in Rus-   0983
sia, Sweden, and Denmark, 1663—1664.   History of Ideas News Letter, 3: 8—17.

Toynbee, Margaret.   Verses on the Louvre.   TLS,   0984
May 17, p. 305.

Wall, L. N.   Marvell and the Third Dutch War.   0985
N&Q, N.S. 4: 296—297.

Wall, L. N.   Some Notes on Marvell's Sources.   0986
N&Q, N.S. 4: 170—173.

1958

Brant, R. L.   Hawthorne and Marvell.   American   0987
Literature, 30: 366.

Davison, Dennis.   Notes on Marvell's "To His   0988

ANDREW MARVELL

Coy Mistress." N&Q, N.S. 5: 521.
0989 Duncan-Jones, E. E. The Date of Marvell's "To
His Coy Mistress." TLS, December 5, p. 705.
0990 Duncan-Jones, E. E. New Allusions to Marvell.
TLS, June 20, p. 345.
0991 Hill, Christopher. Puritanism and Revolution.
London, Secker and Warburg. 402 p.
0992 Hyman, Lawrence W. Marvell's Garden. ELH, 25:
13—22.
0993 Hyman, Lawrence W. Politics and Poetry in Andrew Marvell. PMLA, 73: 475—479.
0994 Legouis, Pierre. Marvell's Grasshoppers. N&Q,
N.S. 5: 108—109.
0995 Lord, George de F. The Case for Internal Evidence.
Two New Poems by Marvell? Bulletin of the
New York Public Library, 62: 551—570.
0996 Press, John. Andrew Marvell. (The British Council). London, Longmans, Green. 42 p.
0997 Putney, Rufus. "Our Vegetable Love": Marvell
and Burton. In Studies in Honor of T. W. Bald-
win, pp. 220—228. Urbana, University of Illinois.
0998 Robbins, Caroline. A Marvell Letter. TLS, December 19, p. 737.
0999 Saveson, J. E. Marvell's "On a Drop of Dew."
N&Q, N.S. 5: 289—290.
1000 Sharrock, Roger. The Date of Marvell's "To His
Coy Mistress." TLS, October 31, p. 625.
1001 Skelton, Robin. Rowland Watkins and Andrew Marvell. N&Q, N.S. 5: 531—532.
1002 Spitzer, Leo. Marvell's "Nymph Complaining for
the Death of Her Faun.": Sources versus Meaning. MLQ, 19: 231—243.
1003 Wall, L. N. Andrew Marvell of Meldreth. N&Q,
N.S. 5: 399—400.
1004 Wall, L. N. A Note on Marvell's Letters. N&Q,
N.S. 5: 111.

1959

1005 Allen, Don Cameron. Love in a Grave. MLN, 74:
485—486.
1006 Allentuck, Marcia E. Marvell's "Pool of Air."

ANDREW MARVELL

MLN, 74: 587—589.

Bain, Carl E.   The Latin Poetry of Andrew Marvell.   1007
PQ, 38: 436—449.

Carroll, John J.   The Sun and the Lovers in "To His   1008
Coy Mistress."   MLN, 74: 4—7.

Coolidge, John S.   Martin Marprelate, Marvell,   1009
and Decorum Personae as a Satirical Theme.
PMLA, 74: 526—532.

Corder, Jim.   Marvell and Nature.   N&Q, N.S. 6:   1010
58—61.

Dodds, M. H.   Rowland Watkins and Andrew Mar-   1011
vell.   N&Q, N.S. 6: 234—235.

Duncan-Jones, E. E.   Marvell, Johnson, and the   1012
First Sunset.   TLS, April 3, p. 193.

Fogel, Ephim G.   The Case for Internal Evidence.   1013
Salmons in Both, or Some Caveats for Canoni-
cal Scholars.   Bulletin of the New York Public
Library, 63: 223—236.

Hill, Christopher.   Andrew Marvell and the Good   1014
Old Cause.   Mainstream, 12: 1—27.

Legouis, Pierre.   Marvell and "the two learned   1015
brothers of St. Marthe."   PQ, 38: 450—458.

Lord, George de F.   The Case for Interal Evi-   1016
dence.   Comments on the Canonical Caveat.
Bulletin of the New York Public Library, 63:
355—366.

Poggioli, Renato.   The Pastoral of the Self.   Daeda-   1017
lus, 88: 686—699.

Robbins, Caroline.   Marvell to Sir Henry Thomp-   1018
son.   TLS, March 20, p. 161.

Røstvig, Maren-Sofie.   Andrew Marvell's "The   1019
Garden": A Hermetic Poem.   English Studies,
40: 65—76.

Schmitter, Dean Morgan.   Marvell's "Treasurer."   1020
N&Q, N.S. 6: 263—264.

Sharrock, Roger.   The Date of Marvell's "To His   1021
Coy Mistress."   TLS, January 16, p. 33.

Sherbo, Arthur.   A Reply to Professor Fogel.   Bulle-   1022
tin of the New York Public Library, 63: 367—
371.

Wall, L. N.   Marvell's Friends in the City.   N&Q,   1023
N.S. 6: 204—207.

ANDREW MARVELL

1960

1024 Alvarez, A.   Marvell and the Poetry of Judgment.
       Hudson Review, 13: 417—428.
1025 Baron, Hans.   Marvell's "An Horatian Ode" and
       Machiavelli. JHI, 21: 450—451.
1026 Colaiacomo, Paola.   Alcuni Aspetti della Poesia di
       Andrew Marvell. English Miscellany, 11: 75—
       111.
1027 Cunningham, James V.   Tradition and Poetic Struc-
       ture. Denver, A. Swallow. 273 p.
1028 Duncan-Jones, E. E.   Marvell and the Song "In
       Guilty Night." TLS, September 8, p. 577.
1029 Hyman, Lawrence W.   Marvell's "Coy Mistress"
       and Desperate Lover. MLN, 75: 8—10.
1030 Legouis, Pierre.   Marvell's "Nymph Complaining
       for the Death of her Faun.": A Mise au Point.
       MLQ, 21: 30—32.
1031 Mazzeo, Joseph A.   Cromwell as Machiavellian
       Prince in Marvell's "An Horatian Ode." JHI, 21:
       1—17.
1032 Millgate, Michael.   The Two Voices of Andrew
       Marvell. Listener, 63: 701—702.
1033 Mitchell, Charles.   Marvell's "The Mower to the
       Glo-Worms." Explicator, 18: 50.
1034 Rosenberg, John D.   Marvell and the Christian
       Idiom. Boston University Studies in English, 4:
       152—161.
1035 Salerno, Nicholas A.   Marvell's "The Unfortunate
       Lover." VIII. Explicator, 18: 42.
1036 Schmitter, Dean Morgan.   The Occasion for Mar-
       vell's Growth of Popery. JHI, 21: 568—570.

KATHERINE PHILIPS

1951

Elmen, Paul. Some Manuscript Poems by the   1037
Matchless Orinda. PQ, 30: 53—57.

THOMAS TRAHERNE

1939

Grandvoinet, Renée. Thomas Traherne and the   1038
Doctrine of Felicity. Études de lettres, 13:
164—177.

1940

Bury, R. G. A Passage in Traherne. TLS, June 8,   1039
p. 279.

Dobell, P. J. A Passage in Traherne. TLS, June   1040
15, p. 291.

1941

Traherne, Thomas. A Serious and Pathetical Con-   1041
templation of the Mercies of God, in Several
Most Devout and Sublime Thanksgivings for the
Same. Edited by R. Daniells. Toronto, Toronto
University. 127 p.

1942

Traherne, Thomas. Of Magnanimity and Charity.   1042
Edited by John R. Slater. New York, King's
Crown. xvi, 20 p.

1944

Huntington, Virginia E. Thomas Traherne, Priest,   1043
Mystic, Poet. Living Church, 109 (December 3):
13—14.

Wade, Gladys I. Thomas Traherne: A Critical   1044
Biography. Princeton, Princeton University.
x, 269 p.

THOMAS TRAHERNE

1945

1045 Bennett, J. A. W. Traherne and Brasenose. N&Q, 189: 84.
1046 Nomachi, Susumu. Thomas Traherne. Studies in English Literature (Tokyo), 24: 154—168.

1947

1047 Colby, Frances L. Thomas Traherne and Henry More. MLN, 62: 490—492.
1048 Gilbert, Allan H. Thomas Traherne as Artist. MLQ, 8: 319—341, 435—447.

1948

1049 Howarth, R. G. "Felicity" in Traherne. N&Q, 193: 249—250.
1050 Traherne, Thomas. Centuries of Meditations. London, P. J. and A. E. Dobell. 327 p.

1950

1051 Ellrodt, Robert. Le Message de Thomas Traherne. Cahiers du Sud, 31: 434—456.
1052 Willy, Margaret E. Life Was Their Cry. London, Evans. 196 p.

1951

1053 Anon. Manuscripts of Thomas Traherne. Bodleian Library Record, 3: 179—180.

1953

1054 Hepburn, Ronald W. Thomas Traherne: The Nature and Dignity of Imagination. Cambridge Journal, 6: 725—734.

1954

1055 Margoliouth, H. M. Traherne's Ordination and Birth-Date. N&Q, N.S. 1: 408.
1056 Salter, K. W. The Date of Traherne's Ordination. N&Q, N.S. 1: 282.

1955

1057 Russell, Angela. The Life of Thomas Traherne.

THOMAS TRAHERNE

RES, N.S. 6: 34—43.

Salter, K. W. Traherne and a Romantic Heresy.   1058
N&Q, N.S. 2: 153—156.

1957

Colie, Rosalie L. Thomas Traherne and the In-   1059
finite: The Ethical Compromise. HLQ, 21: 69—
82.

1958

Marshall, William H. Thomas Traherne and the   1060
Doctrine of Original Sin. MLN, 73: 161—165.

Traherne, Thomas. Thomas Traherne: Centuries,   1061
Poems and Thanksgivings. Edited by H. M.
Margoliouth. 2 vols. Oxford, Clarendon.

Wallace, John M. Thomas Traherne and the Struc-   1062
ture of Meditation. ELH, 25: 79—89.

1959

Bottrall, Margaret. Traherne's Praise of the Cre-   1063
ation. Critical Quarterly, 1: 126—133.

Willy, Margaret E. Thomas Traherne: "Felicity's   1064
Perfect Lover." English, 12: 210—215.

1960

Tanner, Lawrence Melvin. Thomas Traherne's   1065
Centuries of Meditations: A Critical Introduc-
tion with Annotations for the First and Second
Centuries. DA, 20: 3310—3311.

Traherne, Thomas. Centuries. With an introduc-   1066
tion by Hilda Vaughan. London, Faith. 228 p.

Traherne, Thomas. Centuries. Introduction by   1067
John Farrar. New York, Harper. 228 p.

HENRY VAUGHAN

1939

Wagner, Hildegaard.   Das Weltbild Henry Vaughans.   1068
Lengerich, Lengerischer Handelsdruck. 141 p.

1940

Ashton, Helen.   The Swan of Usk: A Historical   1069
Novel. New York, Macmillan. 320 p.
Parker, William R.   Henry Vaughan and His Pub-   1070
lishers. The Library, 4th ser., 20: 401—411.

1941

Attwater, Donald.   Henry Vaughan the Silurist: A   1071
Christian Poet. Catholic World, 153: 594—599.
Hughes, Merritt Y.   The Theme of Pre-Existence   1072
and Infancy in The Retreate. In Renaissance
Studies in Honor of Hardin Craig, pp. 292—308.
Stanford, Stanford University. Also published in:
PQ, 20: 484—500.
Marilla, E. L.   A Critical and Interpretative Study   1073
of Henry Vaughan as a Secular Poet. Abstracts
of Doctoral Dissertations. The Ohio State Uni-
versity, no. 36. pp. 215—220.

1942

Doughty, William L.   Religion Under the Stars: A   1074
Study of the Poetry of Henry Vaughan. The Lon-
don Quarterly and Holborn Review, 167: 347—355.
Hutchinson, F. E.   The Strange Case of Olor Isca-   1075
nus. RES, 18: 320—321.
Lehmann, Ruth P.   Characteristic Imagery in the   1076

Poetry of Henry Vaughan. Summaries of Doctoral Dissertations, University of Wisconsin, 7: 293—294.

1077 Marilla, E. L. Henry Vaughan and the Civil War. JEGP, 41: 514—526.

1078 Martin, L. C. Henry Vaughan and "Hermes Trismegistus." RES, 18: 301—307.

1079 Walley, Harold R. The Strange Case of Olor Iscanus. RES, 18: 27—37.

1943

1080 Allen, Don Cameron. Henry Vaughan's "The Ass." MLN, 58: 612—614.

1081 Editors, The. Vaughan's "Peace." Explicator, 1: 43.

1082 Horton-Smith, L. G. H. Henry Vaughan's Epitaph. N&Q, 185: 203—204, 293.

1083 M., M. The Swan of Usk. More Books: Bulletin of the Boston Public Library, 18: 341.

1084 Simpson, Percy. Henry Vaughan's Epitaph. N&Q, 185: 134—135.

1085 Stewart, Bain Tate. The Meaning of Silex Scintillans. PQ, 22: 79—80.

1944

1086 Allen, Don Cameron. Henry Vaughan's "Salome on Ice." PQ, 23: 84—85.

1087 Hutchinson, F. E. Henry Vaughan's Gravestone. N&Q, 186: 255.

1088 K., M. Vaughan's "Man." Explicator, 2: Q25.

1089 Marilla, E. L. Henry and Thomas Vaughan. MLR, 39: 180—183.

1090 Marilla, E. L. The Significance of Henry Vaughan's Literary Reputation. MLQ, 5: 155—162.

1091 Robertson, Jean. The Use Made of Owen Felltham's "Resolves": A Study in Plagiarism. MLR, 39: 108—115.

1092 Svendsen, Kester. Vaughan's "Man." Explicator, 2: 58.

1945

1093 Childe, Wilfred R. Henry Vaughan. Transactions

of the Royal Society of Literature, 3rd ser., 22:
131—160.

Lehmann, Ruth P. Henry Vaughan and Welsh Po-   1094
etry; A Contrast. PQ, 24: 329—342.

Marilla, E. L. The Religious Conversion of Henry   1095
Vaughan. RES, 21: 15—22.

Thoma, Henry F. The Hermetic Strain in Seven-   1096
teenth-Century English Mysticism. Summaries
of Theses, Harvard University, pp. 344—347.

1947

Cheek, Philip M. The Latin Element in Henry   1097
Vaughan. SP, 44: 69—88.

Hutchinson, F. E. Henry Vaughan: A Life and   1098
Interpretation. Oxford, Clarendon. viii, 260 p.

Marsh, Edward. Henry Vaughan. TLS, July 19,   1099
p. 365.

Nuttall, Geoffrey F. "Unity with the Creation":   1100
George Fox and the Hermetic Philosophy.
Friends Quarterly, 3: 134—143.

Walters, Richard H. Henry Vaughan and the Al-   1101
chemists. RES, 23: 107—122.

1948

Marilla, E. L. A Comprehensive Bibliography of   1102
Henry Vaughan. University, Alabama, University of Alabama. 44 p.

Marilla, E. L. Henry Vaughan to Sir William   1103
Davenant. PQ, 27: 181—184.

Marilla, E. L. Henry Vaughan's Conversion: A   1104
Recent View. MLN, 63: 394—397.

Marilla, E. L. "The Publisher to the Reader"   1105
of Olor Iscanus. RES, 24: 36—41.

Marilla, E. L. The Secular and Religious Poetry   1106
of Henry Vaughan. MLQ, 9: 394—411.

1949

Margoliouth, H. M. A Vaughan Emendation. N&Q,   1107
194: 211.

Paul, Frances. Henry Vaughan. Contemporary Re-   1108
view, 176: 368—372.

HENRY VAUGHAN

1950

1109 Kermode, Frank. The Private Imagery of Henry Vaughan. RES, N.S. 1: 206—225.

1110 Stewart, Bain Tate. Hermetic Symbolism in Henry Vaughan's "The Night." PQ, 29: 417—422.

1951

1111 Erede, Anna. Un Delicato Poeta del Seicento Inglese: Henry Vaughan. Studium, 47: 550—555.

1112 Weir, J. L. Bibliographical Notices of "The Last Battell of the Soule in Death." (1628—1629). N&Q, 196: 76—79.

1952

1113 Smith, H. Rossiter. Medicine and Poetry. N&Q, 197: 423—425.

1114 Stead, William F. Some Unknown Verses by Henry Vaughan? TLS, February 8, p. 116.

1953

1115 Bethell, S. L. The Theology of Henry and Thomas Vaughan. Theology, 56: 137—143.

1116 Martin, L. C. Henry Vaughan and "The Chymists Key." TLS, December 11, p. 801.

1117 Williamson, E. W. Henry Vaughan. London, B.B.C. 40 p.

1954

1118 Allen, Don Cameron. Vaughan's "Cock-Crowing" and the Tradition. ELH, 21: 94—106.

1119 McChesney, John. Vaughan's "The Queer." Explicator, 12: Q3.

1120 Oliver, H. J. The Mysticism of Henry Vaughan: A Reply. JEGP, 53: 352—360.

1121 Røstvig, Maren-Sofie. Casimire Sarbiewski and the English Ode. SP, 51: 443—460.

1122 Røstvig, Maren-Sofie. The Happy Man; Studies in the Metamorphoses of a Classical Ideal 1600—1700. Oslo, Akademisk Forlag. 496 p.

✗ 1123 Wright, Herbert G. The Theme of Solitude and Retirement in Seventeenth Century Literature.

HENRY VAUGHAN

Études Anglaises, 7: 22—35.

1955

Barksdale, Richard K. The Nature Poetry of Henry   1124 ✕
Vaughan. The Western Humanities Review, 9:
341—348.
Emslie, Macdonald. Vaughan's "The Queer." Ex-   1125
plicator, 13: 29.
Gesner, Carol. A Note on Henry Vaughan. MLR,   1126
50: 172—173.
Perrine, Laurence. Vaughan's "The Queer." Ex-   1127
plicator, 13: 29.
Rickey, Mary Ellen. Crashaw and Vaughan. N&Q,   1128
N.S. 2: 232—233.
Wright, Celeste Turner. Vaughan's "The Queer."   1129
Explicator, 13: 29.

1956

Francis, W. Nelson. Vaughan's "The Waterfall."   1130
Explicator, 14: 57.
Hilberry, Conrad. Vaughan's "The Morning Watch." 1131
Explicator, 14: 44.
Pettet, E. C. A Simile in Vaughan. TLS, January   1132
27, p. 53.

1957

Durr, Robert A. Vaughan's Theme and Its Pattern: 1133
"Regeneration." SP, 54: 14—28.
Vaughan, Henry. The Works of Henry Vaughan.   1134
Edited by L. C. Martin. 2nd edn. Oxford,
Clarendon. xxviii, 771 p.

1958

Marilla, E. L. Henry Vaughan. JEGP, 57: 368—369. 1135
Midgley, Graham. Vaughan's Glittering Flint.   1136
TLS, March 7, p. 127.
Raby, F. J. E. Vaughan's Glittering Flint. TLS,   1137
February 28, p. 115.
Vaughan, Henry. The Secular Poems of Henry   1138
Vaughan. Edited by E. L. Marilla (Essays and
Studies on English Language and Literature, 21).
Uppsala, Lundequistska. xvi, 337 p.

HENRY VAUGHAN

1959

1139   Farnham, Fern.   The Imagery of Henry Vaughan's "The Night." PQ, 38: 425—435.

1140   Garner, Ross.   Henry Vaughan; Experience and the Tradition. Chicago, University of Chicago. viii, 176 p.

1960

1141   Durr, Robert A.   Vaughan's "The Night." JEGP, 59: 34—40.

1142   Durr, Robert A.   Vaughan's Pilgrim and the Birds of Night: "The Proffer." MLQ, 21: 45—58.

1143   Howarth, R. G.   Notes on Vaughan. N&Q, N.S. 7: 65—67, 236.

1144   Pettet, E. C.   Of Paradise and Light; A Study of Vaughan's Silex Scintillans. Cambridge, Cambridge University. x, 217 p.

1145   Simmonds, James D.   The Date of Henry Vaughan's "Silex Scintillans." N&Q, N.S. 7: 64—65.

1146   Simmonds, James D.   The Dedication of Henry Vaughan's Silex Scintillans. English Studies, 41: 369.

1147   Simmonds, James D.   The Problem of Henry Vaughan's Illness. Anglia, 78: 353—356.

INDEX OF AUTHORS

AUTHOR INDEX

AUTHOR INDEX

AUTHOR INDEX

AUTHOR INDEX

AUTHOR INDEX